'ORRIBLE MURDER

VICTORIAN CRIME AND PASSION

SELECTIONS FROM THE ILLUSTRATED POLICE NEWS

'ORRIBLE MURDER

AN ANTHOLOGY OF
VICTORIAN CRIME AND PASSION
COMPILED FROM

BY LEONARD DE VRIES

IN COLLABORATION WITH ILONKA VAN AMSTEL
WHO ALSO DESIGNED THE BOOK

TAPLINGER PUBLISHING COMPANY
NEW YORK

First Published in the United States in 1971 by
Taplinger Publishing Co., Inc.
New York, New York

Copyright © Leonard de Vries 1971

International Standard Book Number 0–8008–6120–5
Library of Congress Catalog Card Number 78–134283

Printed in Great Britain

CONTENTS

9 A sanctimonious scoundrel murders his own child 24 5 1879

10 A horrible crime 25 11 1876

Double murder and suicide at Kennington 31 8 1867

12 Horrible tragedy 9 11 1868

Fatal boiler explosion at South Shields 7 7 1877

13 Riots at Ashton under Lyne 23 5 1868

14 Shocking death of a man on a Welsh mountain 11 9 1869

Frightful accident at a stone quarry 7 3 1868

16 Suicide of two girls 24 10 1868

17 Strange and horrible suicide 4 10 1879

18 Exciting scene at a fire 15 6 1867

20 A living woman measured for her coffin 23 7 1870

21 Horrible scene at a wake 26 8 1871

The dead alive 28 9 1872

22 Shutting a woman's head in a box 4 3 1876

Fatal accident at Hull 23 4 1877

Death of a somnambulist 9 2 1878

Shocking suicide at Crystal Palace 25 5 1867

23 A horrible discovery 1 7 1876

Killed by a coffin 9 11 1872

24 Rising from the dead 18 5 1878

Narrow escape from drowning at Brierley Hill 9 11 1872

26 Desperate encounter with an eagle 7 8 1869

A child killed by a pig 17 9 1870

27 A child stolen by a monkey 9 7 1870

Dreadful murder and suicide 19 7 1873

28 A lunatic in a railway train 4 8 1877

29 Murderous attack by a gorilla 22 4 1876

30 Fortune telling at Rotherham 19 5 1877

An encounter with a mad dog at a post office 16 8 1877

Suicide on a railway 23 12 1871

31 An extraordinary suicide 19 8 1876

32 Brutal murder near Crook 8 10 1870

Duel with pistols 24 11 1877

Disastrous floods 12 1 1878

33 Fearful death of three children 21 4 1877

Madness and murder 22 2 1868

Exciting scene 15 4 1876

Fatal accident to a signalman 1 1 1876

34 Fatal encounter with a shark 18 3 1871

Cat's meat man attacked by dogs 26 8 1876

35 Death from swallowing a mouse 15 1 1876

Brutal treatment of a cat 10 7 1869

The execution of Hoedel 31 8 1878

36 An inhuman father 17 11 1877

37 Dreadful child murder at Hull 24 5 1873

38 Attempt to drown a supposed witch 1 7 1876

39 Cruel treatment of an orphan 10 6 1876

Killing a supposed witch 1 1 1876

40 A horrible tale of the sea 26 10 1872

42 Robbing schoolgirls of their wearing apparel 25 11 1871

Loss of a Hull fishing smack 19 5 1877

The Whitechapel tragedy 18 9 1875

43 Attempted murder at Hull 17 11 1877

44 The flying man "Bat" 21 6 1873

45 Killed by a bicycle 4 5 1878

Throwing a wife out of a window 26 10 1872

46 Aeronaut attacked by crocodile 9 2 1878

47 Novel and fatal balloon duel 16 3 1878

48 Fatal accident to children 15 7 1871

Fearful balloon accident 1 7 1871

50 Attempted suicide 14 1 1871

Fatal assault on a woman 21 7 1877

Playing at Wainwright 29 1 1876

51	Suicide of a butcher's wife at Bolton	12	12	1868
52	Fatal case of elephant teasing	27	4	1872
53	Fearful encounter with a boa constrictor	11	8	1877
	Attacked by lions	14	10	1871
54	Appalling scene	10	12	1870
55	Narrow escape of a Lilliputian tiger tamer versus cats	29	1	1876
57	A girl seized by a gorilla	16	12	1876
	Child stealing extraordinary	18	5	1878
58	Found dead in streets	28	7	1877
	Attempted murder on the Thames	23	6	1877
	Barbarous murder	31	8	1867
60	Newgate—Tuesday morning	1	1	1876
61	Execution of Wiggins	19	10	1867
62	Awful cruelty to an idiot boy	10	6	1876
	Killed by a cricket ball	7	7	1877
63	A boy mistaken for a crow	24	6	1876
	Singular fatality	14	4	1877
	Five children thrown into a well	18	4	1868
64	Placing an old woman on the fire	12	11	1870
	Murder at West Bromwich	8	7	1871
66	Destructive fire in the Strand	4	9	1869
67	A cask of whiskey on fire	11	8	1877
68	Miraculous escape from a fire	17	12	1870
	Fearful wife beating	26	9	1868
69	Frightful wife murder in Bristol	11	3	1876
	Fatal quarrel	19	2	1876
70	Hairdressing extraordinary	24	8	1872
	Fearful tragedy of a lunatic stepmother	9	9	1871
71	Children severely flogged	19	2	1877
72	Flogging garrotters at Leeds	18	12	1869
73	A wife driven insane by husband tickling her feet	11	12	1869
74	Singular method of execution	5	7	1873
75	Japanese punishment for adultery	31	7	1875
	Lynching four men	27	9	1873
76	Suicide from Waterloo Bridge	21	9	1872
77	The burning of a ship and five hundred coolies	15	7	1871
79	An encounter with a sea devil	21	6	1873
80	Horrible discovery of a girl eaten by rats	13	8	1870
81	A burglar bitten by a skeleton	27	6	1874
	Shocking treatment of a lunatic	8	4	1876
82	Gross inhumanity to children	23	6	1877
83	The last moments of a gorilla	15	1	1876
85	Thrilling accident at Bolton	15	5	1869
	A ballet girl burnt to death	28	3	1868
86	Suicide from the bridge at Clifton, Bristol	11	9	1869
	The skeleton in the cupboard	8	4	1871
89	A sponge diver swallowed by a sea monster	2	9	1876
90	Terrible suffering of two shipwrecked sailors	11	12	1880
91	Encounter with a ghost	14	12	1872
92	Appalling discovery of two skeletons in a theatre	9	11	1867
93	Singular attempt at suicide	24	6	1876
94	Execution of Troppmann by guillotine	22	1	1870
95	Shocking murder and suicide	1	8	1868
96	Strange intruder in a lady's bedroom	28	12	1872
	Murderous assault	3	11	1877
	Extraordinary scene at a wedding	5	8	1871
98	Another extraordinary scene at a wedding	9	7	1870
	Shocking cruelty	10	6	1876
99	Murderous attack on a woman at Whitney	12	8	1871
100	Awful death struggle	21	6	1873
101	Shocking murder near Grimsby	4	3	1871
102	Murder and mutilation of a woman	12	10	1872
103	Horrible cannibalism	9	12	1871
	Poor Billet the weaver starved to death	21	11	1868
105	Jealousy and revenge in high life	22	7	1871
107	Shocking tragedy in Soho	4	3	1871
108	Dreadful murder at a bank	15	7	1871
109	A baron's cruelty to his wife	6	9	1879
110	Strange discovery	2	11	1872
	Terrible discovery of a skeleton	16	7	1870

112	Life and death of a work girl	20	4	1867
113	Midnight attack at St. Albans	5	10	1867
114	An encounter with a ghost	10	7	1869
	Horrible discovery of a skeleton	4	9	1869
116	Fight with a vulture	29	4	1876
117	Extraordinary discovery of the remains of two persons	23	2	1867
118	Fearful encounter with a boa constrictor	15	4	1871
119	Ludicrous scene	13	8	1870
	The deadly embrace of a devil fish	11	5	1878
	Fatal accident on board ship	8	9	1877
120	Extraordinary scene at a wedding	25	5	1867
121	Fearful adventure with a shark	7	12	1872
122	Extraordinary collection of cats	1	6	1867
123	A man crucifying himself	26	6	1869
124	Fearful cliff adventure	13	1	1877
125	A child saved by a dog	18	11	1876
	Fatal alpine accident	10	7	1880
126	Charge of throwing a woman from a window	26	2	1876
	Double murder and suicide	6	5	1871
128	Boy scalded to death	6	5	1871
129	Romantic suicide	19	8	1876
	The timely warning	5	4	1873
130	Dreadful death	9	2	1868
	Dining off a dead horse	25	2	1871
	Attempted murder and suicide	12	10	1867
132	Revolting cruelty to a dog and cat	11	12	1869
133	Appalling carriage accident on Hackney Marshes	3	8	1867
	Roasting a dog alive	12	2	1876
134	Dead	4	3	1876
	Two prisoners flogged at Newgate	25	11	1871
135	A clergyman flogging a boy	19	8	1871
136	Fearful scene	22	7	1876
	Scene on Plumstead Common	18	11	1876
137	Capital punishments	29	6	1872
139	Cruelty to a daughter	20	5	1876
	Shocking murder at Newcastle	11	2	1871
140	Mysterious death at Penge	2	6	1877
141	Fatal fall from a cliff at Ramsgate	12	8	1871
142	A cold dip	1	4	1876
	Extraordinary wife murder	7	2	1874
	Murderous assault	3	11	1877
143	Attempt to strangle wife	21	7	1877
	Fatal affray at a gaming table	5	8	1871
144	Fatal accident to an impalement performance	25	3	1876
	Zazel shot from a gun	14	4	1877
145	Attempted murder by a son	23	5	1868
147	Extraordinary suicide	22	5	1880
	Murder and attempted suicide	29	7	1871
	Baby farming at Brixton	25	6	1870
148	Cruel treatment of a girl	26	8	1876
149	Shocking cruelty to children	15	7	1876
150	Extraordinary scene in the house of a hermit	22	5	1869
151	Horrible murder by two women	27	11	1886
152	Horrible treatment of a nun	7	8	1869
153	Terrible outrage	25	12	1880
	Fatal balloon accident	27	10	1877
154	Thames mystery	27	9	1873
155	Saved by a kite	30	4	1887
	Shocking accident	8	7	1876
	Death in a bathing machine	12	8	1871
156	Murder and suicide at Salford	30	5	1868
157	Attempted wife murder	16	5	1868
158	A woman raised from the dead	16	3	1878
	Suicide by a guillotine	12	2	1876
159	Attack upon a boy by a dog	6	10	1877
160	Suicide from Waterloo Bridge	29	8	1868

A SANCTIMONIOUS SCOUNDREL MURDERS HIS OWN CHILD

Boston telegrams report intense excitement at Pocasset, Massachusetts. Charles Freeman, member of Second Advent Congregation, recently became insane from excitement at revival meetings. A week ago he declared he had received a wonderful revelation, and has not eaten or slept since. He declared that God had directed him to sacrifice his daughter Edith, aged five, and that she would rise again in three days. He seized her on Thursday and transfixed her with a knife upon the table, improvised as an altar, killing her, and pouring out her blood on the altar. He then drove the horrified family from the house and barricaded the doors and windows. Being well armed he threatened death to anyone who interfered with him. He thus awaited Sunday's resurrection.

A later despatch says Freeman was arrested on Friday afternoon with his wife, and taken to Barnstable Gaol, Cape Cod, where the excitement continues. He killed his child at daybreak on Thursday, his wife assenting, and both praying before the murder. Then he summoned an advent meeting which assembled in the afternoon. He told them of the sacrifice he had made and exhibited the body to the meeting. He endeavoured to keep the sacrifice a secret but it was disclosed. Then he drove everyone from the house. On Friday he conducted an incantation over the body preparatory to Sunday's resurrection. After his arrest, while being taken on the railway to gaol, he sang hymns and declared he was the second Abraham obeying a divine mandate. His wife seconded him and neither expressed anxiety as to the future. Freeman is a farmer in moderate circumstances. The body of his daughter has been taken by the neighbours, who conducted the funeral. Several Adventists at Pocasset who attended the meeting will be arrested as accessories. This crime attracts great attention throughout the country.

BIGOTED SCOUNDRELS—MURDER BY 'SACRIFICE'

A HORRIBLE CRIME

A horrible crime

A diabolical murder has been committed in Spain. The circumstances of the case are as follows: A Spaniard of the name of Paquillo, who is a man between forty and fifty years of age, fell desperately in love with a girl little more than half his age. A mutual warmth sprang up, and Paquillo proposed marriage, but found that the girl had two little children. This, it appears, marred the happiness of both. The lovers were estranged for some time. However, the man was most passionately fond of the girl and very soon a reconciliation took place. A fearful and atrocious crime of a barbaric nature was determined on. **While the two children were peacefully slumbering Paquillo entered their bed-chamber, and plunged a dagger in their breasts, the mother the while calmly looking on. The guilty parties have fled no one knows whither.**

DOUBLE
MURDER AND SUICIDE AT KENNINGTON

On Friday morning at an early hour numbers of persons visited the house where the dreadful occurrence took place on Thursday, for the purpose of trying to get a look at the rooms, but orders had been given to the police to admit none until the coroner opened the inquest. The crowd divided into small groups and every item of intelligence was eagerly sought after and discussed, but it is needless to say that the statements made under such circumstances were not of the most reliable character. It is stated that Mrs. Roberts had for some time past been brooding over some imaginary wrong. The mother of the wretched woman died raving mad. The crime it is thought, was premeditated, for the deceased waited until all the lodgers in the house had left before she killed her children.

The Inquest

On Friday afternoon, Mr. William Carter, coroner, opened an investigation at the Sir Sydney Smith Tavern, Chester-street, touching the deaths of Mrs. Anne Roberts and her two children, Frederick and Anne Maria.

Mr. Inspector Heath, of the L division, attended to watch the proceedings on behalf of the police, and the Court and its approaches were densely crowded.

Charles Roberts was the first witness and cried bitterly while giving his evidence. He said: My father's name is Charles and he is a builder and decorator of houses. I lived with him and my mother. My mother's name was Anne Maria Roberts and her age was forty. My sister Anne was aged nine years and my brother Frederick seven years. On Thursday afternoon between four and five o'clock, my mother said she would do for us. I was then in the back garden with Reuben Ashley, a lad between ten and eleven. My brother Frederick was playing with me and my mother called out

"Frederick I want you". Freddy did not go at first and my mother called a second time and said "Freddy, why don't you hear". He went upstairs and I followed him and washed my hands. I heard a scraping noise on the floor of the lumber room overhead, and went up to the door. It was locked. I heard a sound like the pouring of water in the back room, and I heard my mother's voice. I said what is the matter and my mother said "She is very ill". My mother then rushed out of the room and went into the other room, where my sister Anne was. She cut at her two or three times. There was no resistance on the part of my sister. I then ran away and my mother followed me. I ran into the front garden and called out "Murder" and "Police". I did so because she said in the afternoon she would kill herself. I did not then say anything to her. The boy who was with me in the garden told her not to be a foolish woman, and I believed she would do something to herself.

Reuben Ashley, a lad referred to by last witness, gave corroborative evidence.

Mrs. Elizabeth Hills said: My husband is a mathematical instrument maker, and lives at 53, Chester Street. On the afternoon in question I was in my back garden between half past four and five o'clock. I heard cries of "Murder" and "Police". The voice appeared to come from Mr. Roberts, at the back of her house. I called out, but receiving no reply I went to the front and Charles Roberts came out and said "She has killed the two children and stabbed herself". I ran into the house by the front door and found Mrs. Roberts lying in the kitchen just before the fire, with a knife in her hand. She was about falling, and did fall. I asked her what she had done—she tried to speak and could not—I did not see anything the matter with her when she fell but afterwards saw she had a large cut above the elbow joint and blood was flowing from it. The child Anne was lying on the floor beside the bed. In the other room on the floor, I saw the boy Frederick. Both were bleeding from wounds in the throat. Mrs. Roberts did not speak to me afterwards.

Some Police evidence was taken as to the bodies and premises. Mr. Wheeler, Surgeon, of Kennington Park Road, said he was called to the place, and in the kitchen found the deceased woman with a wound 3″ long in the left arm. In the upstairs room he found the body of the boy with a large gash in the throat. He then went into the front room and saw the body of the little girl who had a wound in her throat and was quite dead.

The Coroner said the question now arose whether the deaths of the children were the result of an act of violence on the part of another party and, if so, was that party the mother of the children.

The jury said they were unanimously of the opinion that the mother had caused the death of the children, and they at once returned a verdict of "Wilful Murder" against Anne Maria Roberts, the mother, in both cases.

The Coroner said he would now take the evidence as to the death of Mrs. Roberts herself. Several witnesses were examined and the jury after twenty minutes deliberation returned a verdict "That the deceased Anne Maria Roberts, having wilfully murdered her two children, destroyed her own life whilst in a state of unsound mind".

The proceedings then terminated and the crowd soon after dispersed.

HORRIBLE TRAGEDY THE MURDER OF A WHOLE FAMILY

The following account of the murder of eight persons is translated from a German paper.

An unheard of crime was perpetrated in August last year by Timm Thode, a peasant's son, 23 years of age who murdered with unequalled barbarity, his whole household, viz his parents, his four brothers, his sister and a maid-servant. Timm Thode's confession, made without any sign of repentence, gives a full explanation of his motive and mode of carrying out the execution of the crime. The plan he had for killing one after another of them in their beds he gave up as he was afraid the noise would awaken the rest, and he would not arrive at the wished for result. On the 6th August he had already laid to hand a six foot long hand spike to kill his brothers with and he struck them one after the other from behind. Now his father must be disposed of. Timm, by telling him the oxen had broken loose, gets him down in front of the front door and strikes him down in front of the farm yard. He brings the remains of his father back to the house in a cart and removes the stains of blood by digging up the earth.

Now follows an account of a terrible combat in a room between sister and brother. The mother lies on the floor, stunned by a blow from the hatchet. The sister springs out of bed in order to save the mother. He strikes out at the sister with a knife and then kills her with the hatchet. Finally he runs to the servant girl's room, feels about for the bed head in the darkness, strikes upon it twice with the hatchet and the last murder is accomplished. The girl dies without a sound. "There I have them all dead" are his only words. He then set fire to the barn to conceal his deed and places the corpses in such a way that they must be destroyed at the breaking out of the fire. The conflagration was however discovered too early and Thode in the course of the examination was driven to confess the crime. Timm Thode was brought to trial and condemned to death. The condemned man left the Court with indescribable placidity.

TIMM'S ATTEMPT TO CUT THE DOG'S THROAT.

HORRIBLE TRAGEDY—THE MURDER OF A WHOLE FAMILY.
TIMM'S ATTACK ON HIS BROTHERS.

THE MURDER OF HIS MOTHER AND SISTER.

Fatal Boiler Explosion at South Shields

On Friday afternoon, last week, an explosion occurred at the Tyne Plate Glass Works, South Shields, by which two persons lost their lives. The section of the premises extends along the riverside and the catastrophe occurred on the frontage of two hundred yards from the Penny Ferry up to the Mill Dam. The easternmost portion of the works is devoted to the making of smelting pots, mixing rooms, furnaces and casting floors, while at the west end are the grinding sheds, and it was in conjunction with this latter portion that the accident took place. The machinery in the lower grinding shed is driven by a pair of horizontal engines of 24 inch cylinders. The boiler stack from which the motive power was obtained is situated outside, at the northwest corner of the lower shed, being built with the fire ends of the boilers facing the river, and the sides of the boilers being parallel with the "gut" termed Mill Dam. The stack comprised four boilers, made of iron each measuring thirty feet by five feet in diameter, and each boiler was securely embedded in stone brickwork. The requirements of the works were not sufficient to warrant all four boilers being in use at once.

It appears that while the grinding sheds were in full operation, and the large body of men, boys and women employed in the manufacture and preparation of plate-glass, were following their usual employment, a sudden dull, heavy report, followed by dense volumes of steam and smoke, and the crashing in of the river end of the lowest grinding shed, gave warning that some alarming accident had taken place. As soon as the smoke and dust and been cleared away it became clear that No. 3 boiler had exploded with a terrific force, carrying away nearly the whole end of the shed, and sending a considerable portion of the masonry and brickwork flying in all directions. A portion of the boiler measuring twenty-six feet in length was lifted bodily out of its bed and sent in a westerly direction over the Mill Dam, a distance of about 150 yards, while the body itself was thrown in a southerly direction into the shed. The larger of the two fragments was precipitated into the corner of a large tenemented house and the room in which this ponderous mass alighted was occupied by Mr. James Farrell, a compositor, who had just at that moment put his child Anne Farrell, fifteen months, into her cradle. It crashed through the roof and fell upon the child, killing her instantly. The father miraculously escaped with a grazed knee. The egg end of the boiler crashed through the timer shed killing John Slater nine years of age. Several more people were injured but all are now making progress towards recovery.

RIOTS AT ASHTON UNDER LYNE

On Sunday week the Borough of Ashton under Lyne was the scene of great rioting and disturbance arising out of the spirit engendered between the English Protestants and the Irish Romanists, by the fiery harangues of an anti-Popery lecturer. A junction of processions from Dunkinfield, Stalybridge and Ashton having been formed, two of the principal Irish quarters of Ashton were attacked, and a

RIOTS AT ASHTON UNDER LYNE

BOILER EXPLOSION—SOUTH SHIELDS

Frightful Accident at a Stone Quarry

On Thursday morning a frightful accident befel a man named Thomas Burrows, 34 years of age, while engaged in dislodging stone at a quarry of Mountsorrel Granite Company in Leicester. The face of the rock where deceased was at work is very high and it would seem that on Thursday morning blasting operations had been carried on near to the top of the rock, and deceased was ordered to dislodge several large lumps of stone which had become detached by the force of the explosion. In carrying out this operation it is usual for the men to be secured by a rope, and let down from the top by means of a crane. Deceased, however, did not adopt this precaution. He was engaged with a crowbar trying to turn over a piece of stone, weighing from a ton to a ton and a half, when he missed his balance and fell to the bottom of the quarry, the stone falling on top of him cutting his body in two, and mutilating him in a shocking and sickening manner. It was with some difficulty that the stone could be removed by his comrades.

collision took place of a most furious nature. Stones were flying in all directions and after some tough fighting the English withdrew. The rioters then ran to St. Mary's Chapel and commenced to break all the windows but revolvers were fired through from the inside and this prevented the rioters from approaching too closely. The fury of the rioters now seemed to have spent itself and they gradually deserted the streets and went home.

SHOCKING DEATH OF A MAN ON A WELSH MOUNTAIN

At the Dolgelly workhouse, on Tuesday last week, an inquest was held on the body of a man unknown, which had been found by a farmer named John Williams, on Cader Idris mountain, in an advanced state of decomposition, jammed in a hole between two crags. The fleshy part of the head and upper part of the body were all eaten away, which rendered identification almost impossible; but from what was left of the clothes and a small bundle found by the body, it is almost certain that it was the remains of a poor man, a stranger, who was seen begging at the nearest farmhouses, on the last Dolgelly fair day the 9th August.

At the inquest Williams said I live at Bwlchcock. I found the body of a man on Sunday, about six o'clock in the evening. I was then on the mountain looking after the sheep. I found him on that part of the Cader mountain in the parish of Dolgelly. He was in a "carleg" or heap of rough stones; his body from his waist down in a hole and his head and breast out. He had no hat on his head and the greater part of his body had been eaten away. There was a cap lying a yard or two from his body. The lower part of the body was jammed quite fast between the stones. I have no recollection of having seen the man alive, but from enquiries I have made I have no doubt the body is that of an old man who was seen at the neighbouring farmhouses on the 9th August, selling pins and needles, and who had some food at one or two of them. A young lad who was on that day on the mountain, a son of Peter Price of Fronolan, had spoken to an old man on the mountain a little nearer to Cader Idris than the place where the body was found. The boy asked him where he was going in that direction and he answered to Machynlleth. The boy

SHOCKING DEATH ON A WELSH MOUNTAIN

told him he was quite in a wrong path, and pointed out to him which way to go. The old man went in the direction pointed out to him and I have no doubt he met his death by falling into a hole and becoming too fast between the crags to get away. He was quite fast and his hips were jammed tight. We was obliged to put a rope round his legs to haul him up he was jammed so tight. A police constable examined deceased pockets, and found some food there, pieces of oatmeal cakes. He also found 2/11d. in money upon him. He had also with him a small bundle of pins and needles.

Verdict: "Found dead on Cader Idris Mountain; name of the person not known."

SUICIDE OF TWO GIRLS

A deplorable mystery of London was investigated by a Coroner's jury on Monday last. The report of which will be found below.

Early on Friday morning a lock-keeper, not far from the Queen's Road Bridge over the Regent's Canal at Dalston heard screams and splashing in the water. Going at once to the spot with the drags, he, after some delay drew out the dead body of a girl. Meanwhile the police also became aware that there had been a suicide at the bridge and set to work in search of the bodies and by and by they brought out two young women, stark and dead, the hand of one clutching with a convulsive grip, the hair of the other. Of the three unhappy creatures, none of them more than 17 or 18, little is known except that, as they lie rigid and still on the deadhouse table, their sodden garments seem to indicate that they were once "respectable ser-

SUICIDE OF

vants''. Once! for those humble, laborious, honest days were over, and the night before the suicide was spent—as the respectable and virtuous do not spend their nights. At a late hour the three unfortunate girls had been seen sitting in the street, drinking from a bottle; trying, it may be, to drown the cruel memory of the past, or forget the misery of the present, or nerve themselves for their leap into the future—for already the threats of self murder were on their lips. Then they were seen upon the bridge, sitting on the parapet. One threw some papers to another young girl not far off with the request they be taken to her father and that they should tell him

"Esther was with me''. They then joined hands and clasped each other's waists; and the water and the night hid the last wrestle these three girls—not yet much more than children—with a life that was too hard for them. They must no doubt have been wicked; most reprehensible and shocking in the eyes of all proper persons. And yet, perhaps, the rush into the unknown was prompted by something like repentant horror at what they knew —perhaps being bad enough already, they chose to die rather than grow worse, and that is a choice which even the righteous would not always find it easy to make.

Strange and Horrible SUICIDE

The St. Petersburg ZEITUNG publishes the following account of a suicide recently committed in the town of Jhitomir under exceptionally appalling circumstances.

A few days ago a well-dressed traveller arrived at an hotel in that city, stating that he was a colonial agent and that he wished to stay for a short time. A room on the second floor of the hotel was assigned to him and he spent two or three days walking about the streets although the weather was unusually wet and

TWO GIRLS

stormy. On the fourth evening he retired early and locked himself in his room. Next morning after futile knocking at the door and receiving no reply the proprietor became alarmed and caused the door to be broken open. A terrible spectacle presented itself to the assembled household. **The man's body was lying on the bedstead in a state of nudity, its left hand pressed to its heart and the right hand convulsively clutching the hair. An oppressive odour as of scorched fat pervaded the room. No wound was obvious upon the body but the** chest was transversely barred in several places by dull red stripes. A deep and broad burn was exhibited in the middle of the back and the spine was found to be completely carbonised.

Upon the floor beneath the bedstead, were discovered the wicks of three candles which had been embedded in a little blotch of cold stearine, and fixed upon the planking in a layer of melted grease. Over the flame of these candles the man had laid upon the bedstead and suffered his spine to be slowly consumed until he died.

EXCITING SCENE AT A FIRE

Narrow Escape of Six Persons

At an early hour on Saturday morning, a scene of an exciting character occurred in Birmingham. Smoke was slowly filling a house in Newtown-row, and must have noiselessly suffocated the inmates, but that one of them happened fortunately to be awake, and communicated the alarm to the others. The house was the

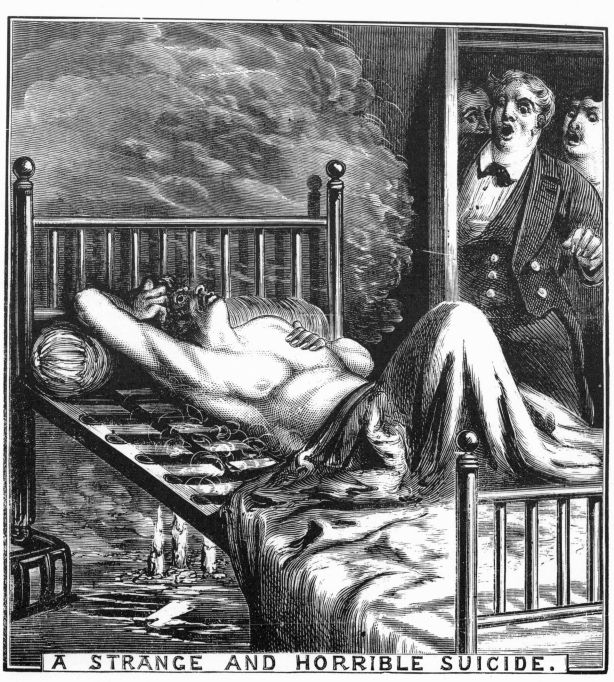

A STRANGE AND HORRIBLE SUICIDE.

residence of Mr. James Ede, draper. A fire had broken out in his shop and the smoke and flames were gradually filling the house, which adjoined the shop. Mrs. Ede was awake; she aroused her husband. Seeing that the premises were on fire he looked about anxiously for a way to escape. He got out through the window and in going along the roof he slipped through a skylight, and his foot was badly wounded. Recovering his self-possession as quickly as possible, he assisted his wife out of the window with her baby, and going along the roof of his own and of an adjoining shop, he and his charges gained access to a neighbouring house, the inmates of which were aroused, and admitted the party who so suddenly claimed shelter and hospitality. But this was not all. There still remained three persons sleeping in Mr. Ede's house, and the fire was every moment gaining ground, and threatening to consume not only the shop, but the dwelling house also.

The three persons thus imperilled were Mr. William Ede, his wife and a female servant. By vigorous cries of "Fire!" the alarm was happily communicated to them. Mr. William Ede, being aroused, jumped out through a window in the rear of the house and ran for a ladder with which to rescue the other inmates. He got the ladder and placed it to the window, and was briskly and hopefully making his way up it. when it broke. A moment of despair, and then a courageous, ingenious device, promptly put into execution. A wall ran close to the window. Mr. William Ede could not jump on to it, nor could the servant. To attempt it was to incur the imminent risk of being killed by a fall. **But Mr. William Ede could bridge the chasm with his body, and he did it. He rested his feet on the window sill and clung with his hands to the wall, and his wife passed over him and the servant followed. Thus all were safe, apparently.** The fire engines arrived and seeing no prospect of being able to save the shop or anything in it, the firemen directed their attention to the premises on either side. While they were at work Mr. William Ede bethought him that a £20 note lay in the pocket of his overcoat inside the burning building, and he reckoned it would not be a bad stroke of business if he could save the coat and the note for a sovereign. The sum was accordingly offered for the recovery of the coat, and a young man tempted by the golden prospect, ventured to enter the house, but returned without success and almost suffocated.

Recovering his breath and animated by the thought of the bright reward in store for him if he could recover the precious coat, he tried again, but was again baffled. Once more he tried, and entered, and fetching his breath hard, and groping about in corners where he could not see, he was thrilled by the touch of a coat. The prize was within the young man's grasp—the sovereign was his. But when he assayed to pull the coat out, he felt that it contained something much heavier and larger than a twenty-pound note. **Dragged to light, it was found to contain, instead of the coveted paper-money the senseless body of Mr. James Ede, who had gone to alarm his brother and his brother's wife and servant, and in the attempt was almost suffocated. In the hurry and confusion no one knew that he was** missing and in danger. As soon as he regained consciousness he was sent in a cab to the General Hospital, as he required treatment, not merely for the exhaustion he suffered, but also for the very severe wound he had received in the foot when he fell through the skylight, but which he disregarded so long as his efforts were necessary for the safety of others.

A LIVING WOMAN MEASURED FOR HER COFFIN

The particulars of a most extraordinary case reaches us from Newtown, an account of which has appeared in many of the local papers in and around the immediate locality. It appears that a middle aged man named Halibane, who is in comparatively easy circumstances, and who resides in the town in question, has had for sometime past a sort of morbid feeling with respect to the disposal of bodies after death, and being under the impression that his days were numbered he made a number of arrangements of an exceptional character for his funeral; and to make sure that these would be carried out he entrusted two of his oldest friends with the charge of superintending his funeral, one of these being an undertaker and the other the Parish clerk. A coffin was made for the eccentric Mr. Halibane which, upon being sent home, did not quite meet with his approval and several alterations were made and eventually the last receptacle for the dead was satisfactory to its future tenant.

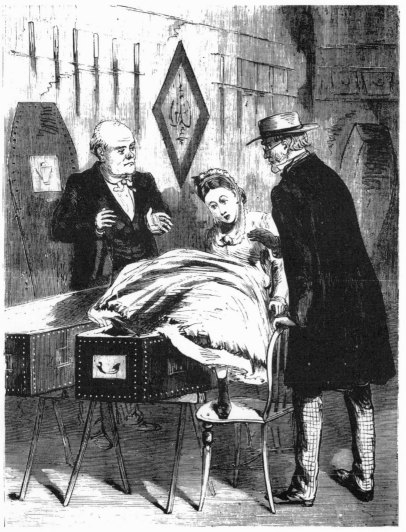

Months passed over, when much to his surprise, the hypochondriacal Mr. Halibane found himself alive and well. He does not appear to have become dispossessed of the idea that he was soon to pass away from the living things of the earth. He now became anxious about his wife, who is an interesting looking young woman, many years his junior. **He persuaded her to be measured for a coffin which was placed by the side of the one made for Mr. Halibane. The capricious gentleman when he saw it at the undertakers, maintained that the last made coffin was too small for his beloved wife, and to demonstrate this fact more clearly, he called upon the undertaker with Mrs. Halibane, and insisted upon her getting at once into the coffin. She hesitated, whereupon her husband grew furious and to pacify him, she placed herself at once in the gloomy receptacle for the dead. In a few minutes she was so completely overcome by the situation in which she found herself, that she fainted and was ultimately conveyed home in a prostrate condition; and from the last accounts received, she has not yet recovered from the effects of the shock to the system. Such are the leading facts of this remarkable case.**

HORRIBLE SCENE AT A WAKE

On Monday morning about three o'clock, the attention of the police was attracted by cries of agony to the house of a man named Daniel Dover, where a horrible scene presented itself. A little boy, two years old, the child of a lodger named Patrick Marron, had died of measles, and a "wake" had been held on the body by several Irishmen. The body was laid upon a table with a lighted candle in each corner, in the living room, and a sheet was stretched from the floor to the joists, and the guests sat around with their pipes and glasses, which they enjoyed as usual on such occasions, and retired at about half-past two. The landlord and the rest of the inmates went to bed, but Marron, like the rest, having indulged rather too freely, and in spite of his wife's pleading, would not allow the candles which were placed round the body, to be extinguished, but would persist in sitting there until they burnt out.

About three o'clock Dover, the landlord, who slept in the room above, was awoke by a sickening smell, and rushing downstairs found that the sheet around the body had caught fire and the flames had reached the joist above. The father was sitting asleep in a stupefied state from the fumes. Great excitement ensued and no time was lost in tearing down the burning sheet and quenching the fire which was fast spreading, and throwing the burning things out of the window. **The corpse presented a sickening spectacle, the fingers and toes being burnt to a cinder, while the body was completely roasted.** Had it not been for the timely awakening it is probable the house would have been completely destroyed by flames.

The Dead Alive

A ludicrous scene occurred on Saturday night in the domicile of a well known undertaker at Hadlay. The tradesman in question (albeit his calling is dismal and depressing enough) is acknowledged by his friends to be of a genial and convivial disposition. He is reputed to be fond of society—and not infrequently indulges in "potations pottles deep". It would appear that on Saturday he had made so frequent use of the bottle as to be so completely overcome that he was not able to reach his own home. He was found by two or three

HORRIBLE SCENE AT A WAKE

of his boon companions in a helpless and almost insensible condition with his legs in a dry ditch, and the upper portion of his body resting against a wall, which stood within twenty yards or so of his house. While in this helpless condition he was taken home by his friends (if such a term could with propriety be applied to them), who, by the way of a practical joke, encased him in one of his own coffins. This done, they took their departure.

The coffin in question had been prepared for a body which was expected to arrive from London in a

shell. Hour after hour passed, and the occupant of the narrow tenement slept on as calmly as if he were in his own bed. In the same room was his wife, seated at a table, reading a ponderous volume. The good lady was perfectly unconscious of the close proximity of her husband. **Her surprise and horror may be readily imagined, when the latter, awakening from his temporary trance, pushed aside the lid which had been loosely laid on the coffin, and gazed with unfeigned surprise at his better half.**

THE DEAD ALIVE

SHUTTING A WOMAN'S HEAD IN A BOX

A case of shocking brutality was heard at Durham on Saturday. George Robson, a miner, pushed his wife's head into a box whilst she was getting her clothes, and held her in that position some minutes then felled her, and putting her head between his legs, broke her jaw-bone. He then turned upon his daughter, twelve months old, and lifted her up by the ears. The magistrates characterized the offence as dreadful brutality and inflicted a sentence of six month's imprisonment.

Death of a Somnambulist

Madame Brouneau, the wife of M. F. Brouneau, of the Dancing Academy, Rivoli House, Belfast, during her sleep on Tuesday night walked out on the roof, fell down into the yard, and was killed. It was stated at the inquest on Wednesday, that the deceased lady was a somnambulist, and a verdict of accidental death was returned.

FATAL ACCIDENT AT HULL

On Friday morning a youth named Robert Chester, an apprentice on board the smack "Times" belonging to Mr. J. Loram, which at the time was lying in the lock-pit of the Albert Dock, was killed by being struck on the forehead with the handle of a winch as he was slackening a rope attached to it. He was struck to the deck and never moved again.

SHOCKING SUICIDE AT CRYSTAL PALACE

Mr. Carter, the coroner for East Surrey held an inquest on the body of the workman who, on Thursday, jumped from the North Water Tower of the Crystal Palace. It was testified that the deceased was forty-three years of age and had been employed as a workman by the Crystal Palace Company, off and on, during eleven years. His occupation on Thursday was with a gang of men collecting the broken iron, so that it could be weighed, from the ruined end of the Palace, near Rockhills, where the great fire had been. They were working at the base of the Water

Tower and Carter was standing on the rail that surrounds the gallery at the base of the great tank. He shouted loudly "Goodbye chaps", threw his cap into the air and sprang from the gallery The height from which he had fallen was 220 feet and his corpse was horribly mutilated. For some days previously he had been very despondent and had been on the drink.

On Thursday morning when he left home his wife remarked that he particularly kissed her and the youngest of his five children, to whom he said "Goodbye". This was unusual with him.

The jury, after some deliberation, returned a verdict—"That the deceased destroyed his own life by leaping from the top of the North Water Tower of the Crystal Palace, while in a state of temporary insanity".

A HORRIBLE DISCOVERY

On Thursday a nauseous odour offended the nostrils of the passengers and others in the station of Hermable-sous-Huy, near Liege in Belgium. It was found to proceed from a large black trunk on which only the name of the station could be found in writing. The commissaire of police was sought for, and on his arrival the package was opened, and in it was the body of a murdered woman, who had been cut up to piecemeal. Where this murderous package came from its not known.

HORRIBLE DISCOVERY

KILLED BY A COFFIN

A report of this melancholy and fatal event was given in our edition of last week. Since then our artist has paid a visit to the cemetery and made a sketch of the scene where the accident occurred, and also a description of the paraphernalia of death, etc.

Dr. Lankester held an inquest at University College Hospital on the body of Henry Taylor, aged sixty-six. The evidence of Mr. E. J. Reading, an undertaker's foreman, and others, showed that on the 19th instant, deceased, with others, was engaged in a funeral at Kensal Green Cemetery. The Church service having been finished, the coffin and mourners, proceeded in coaches towards the place of burial. The day being damp, the foreman directed the coaches, with the mourners, to proceed to the grave by the footway, and the hearse across the grass towards a gravedigger who was motioning the nearest way. The coffin was moved from the hearse and being carried down a path only three feet by six wide, by six bearers, when orders were given to turn, so that the coffin, which is known in the trade as a 4 lb. leaden one, should go head first. While the men were changing it is supposed that deceased caught his foot against a stone and stumbled: **the other bearers, to save themselves, let the coffin go, and it fell with great force onto deceased, fracturing his jaw and ribs. The greatest confusion was created amongst the mourners who witnessed the accident, and the widow of the person to be buried nearly went into hysterics. Further assistance having been procured, the burial service was proceeded with, while deceased was conveyed to a surgery, and ultimately to hospital where he expired. The jury recommended that straps be placed round coffins, which would tend to prevent such accidents. Verdict—accidental death.**

RISING FROM THE DEAD

Reports of a startling occurrence have just come to light from Paterson, N.J. which are the topics of conversation everywhere in that city. On Tuesday last, a daughter of Mr. D. J. Demarest, a grocer, of No. 35, Willis Street, died, it was supposed from heart disease. On Friday the father

RISING FROM THE DEAD.

KILLED BY A C

left the coffin, by the side of which he had been kneeling, and passed to an adjoining room where he threw himself onto an armchair and, weeping, hid his face in his hands. Suddenly he heard, or thought he heard, the patter of a familiar foot-fall, and looking up saw, to his great surprise, the door to the adjoining room softly opened, and the child dressed in her shroud, entering. **She tottered across the room to where he sat, and throwing herself upon his knee twined her arms about his neck.** Then she nestled down in his arms and fell slowly backwards. He lifted her up, but the vital spark had flown. The first semblance of her death had been a trance. The little dead body was interred on that day.

NARROW ESCAPE FROM DROWNING AT BRIERLEY HILL

It is our painful duty to place upon record a serious accident which occurred on Sunday at Clent, and one which might, had providence not otherwise ordained, have given the inhabitants of Brierley Hill cause to bewail the loss of a gentleman who is well known to the general public.

It appears on the day referred to a youthful couple proceeded to Clent, and took up their headquarters in a house whose hospitable shelter is always willingly accorded to such as are willing to remunerate the proprietor with a moderate payment. The happy couple after regaling themselves with the good fare with which the house was well provided, and having recovered from the fatigue of their journey to this place of rustic seclusion, began to perambulate the grounds in the immediate vicinity. Buth their happiness was not attained in the eyes of a third person (a gentleman the one we have above referred to) who had arrived at the

IN AT KENSAL GREEN CEMETERY.

same place of abode, being exceedingly upright and virtuous himself, harboured grave suspicion regarding the ecstatic joys which the company of each other afforded the ingenuous and devoted couple. His mind was tormented with grave anxieties at their being allowed to wander at will, and alone, in the solitude of these pastoral shades. After meditating for some time he sprang up, put on high beaver hat, and strolled out of the house.

This remarkable gentleman, with a truly philanthropic regard for the welfare of young people, followed them over the hills of Clent and amongst the trees. As may be easily imagined, the young couple retraced their steps with all speed. The vigilant spy then being obliged to relinquish the task he had set himself, hurried towards the house from which he had come. Careering along, with his head thrown back and his white collar standing up, he failed to exercise that care in regard to his footsteps which such uncertain ground rendered necessary, and with all the startling suddenness of magic he dropped into the bowels of the earth,

where he was immersed up to the chin in water. He "splashed and dashed" not like a fish, but with the

frantic energy of Johnny Saud's dauntless spouse. After repeated efforts he succeeded in extricating himself from his uncomfortable position; after which he took himself to the comfortable place of abode from which he had already started.

The man altogether from his melancholy appearance and woeful exterior betrayed a sense of the fact that his indescretion had brought upon him a well merited chastisement. The humane landlord put him to bed with all haste while a sweep undertook to dry the clothes for a pecuniary consideration to be settled by the drenched sufferer on the following morning.

DESPERATE ENCOUNTER WITH AN EAGLE

A most miraculous escape from the talons of an eagle is reported in several of the French newspapers. Some children were playing at the base of Mount St. Gothard, when all at once a prolonged scream from their little throats occasioned some alarm to a carpenter who rushed out of his cottage, hatchet in hand, and to his dismay beheld a little boy between three and four years of age being carried off by an eagle. The voracious bird seemed to have some difficulty soaring aloft with its prey. The carpenter began to despair but with rapid strides he ascended the mountain and eventually succeeded in striking one of the eagle's wings a blow with his hatchet. The wounded

bird wavered and began slowly to descend. The carpenter managed to lay hold of the child's clothing and endeavoured to drag the little fellow away, but the eagle retained a firm hold and it was not until he struck it further blows on the leg that it released its prey. The child was in no way injured but the agony of the mother who witnessed the conflict is easier to imagine than to describe.

A CHILD KILLED BY A PIG

One of the most painful circumstances which it has been our duty to record, occurred at Barn-hill near Hacketstown on Friday, resulting in the death of the male infant child of a farmer

named Browne. It appears that the mother went in company with her daughter and servant, to milk cows, after placing the child in bed and latching the door. Soon she was attracted by the cries of the servant and on rushing out of the cow house saw the sow with the child in its mouth running to its stye. She immediately followed and rescued the mangled remains of her infant who died immediately from the injuries inflicted. As there was no person in the house at the time it was evident that the sow had been able to unlatch the door. At the inquest the following day the coroner commented upon the danger of leaving young children without proper care, a practice, unfortunately, too prevalent, and often fraught with fearful consequences.

A CHILD STOLEN BY A MONKEY

A local paper reports a somewhat remarkable case of purloining a child, which occurred in the small village of Manxbridge, in Somersetshire, on Monday last. It appears that Mr. Judcote, a gentleman of independent means, has for a long time past kept a large monkey, who has been accustomed to range over his master's garden and grounds, as the creature was esteemed harmless, and to use a sporting phrase, "was esteemed to be free from vice".

On Monday last, Mrs. Hemmingway, near neighbour of Mr. Judcote, while walking in her garden, was surprised and horrified at beholding "Hulch" Mr. Judcote's monkey, suddenly snatch her baby from the arms of her youngest sister Clara who, as a special favour, had been permitted to take charge of the infant. The monkey gibbering and chattering, rushed off with its prize, and gained the roof of an outhouse with very little difficulty. Mrs. Hemmingway was driven to the utmost extremity of despair, and she vainly strove to repossess herself of her last born. She beheld, to her infinite horror, the monkey pass over the roof of the outhouse, until he and his burden were both lost to sight. The anxious

mother at once hastened to the house of her neighbour Mr. Judcote, who appeared to be as much troubled as herself at the unlooked for disaster. His man servants were despatched in every direction in search of "Hulch" who was, however, too wary to allow his hiding place to be discovered. In the meantime the parents of the child were kept in a constant state of anxiety and trepidation. It was impossible to say what had befallen the child. The day passed without any news of either "Hulch" or the infant, and it was by the merest chance that both the fugitives were discovered by some farm labourers in an adjacent wood towards eight o'clock in the evening. At this time "Hulch" seemed to be tired of his companion, whom he purposely resigned to the farm servants. The delight of the parents upon regaining their child may be more readily imagined than described.

DREADFUL MURDER AND SUICIDE

A dreadful murder was committed at Knowle on Wednesday last week, under circumstances of the most painful character. The details of the shocking tragedy are of a peculiarly distressing nature from the fact that they appear to have been the result of drink caused by domestic unhappiness. The murderer has hitherto borne a most irreproachable character and has occupied a very respectable position in society. He appears to have been drinking on Monday and returned rather late to his home. He rose early in the morning and went out, as it was thought to business, but it is believed instead he went out and got drunk. He returned home about eight o'clock, asked for his breakfast, which was supplied to him by his wife and he ate of it rather heartily. At that time the unhappy child who was murdered was still in bed and he told his wife that he would take her up some sweets. He accordingly went upstairs and remained there for a few minutes during which time he must have cut the girl's throat with his razor whilst she was sleeping.

Not suspecting anything was wrong, Mrs. Abbott continued to busy herself about the house for about a quarter of an hour, when she went upstairs to wake the child for school. **The sight that confronted her was appalling. She uttered a piercing scream, snatched the child up in her arms and rushed into the street.** The murderer was eventually found at the Roman Catholic Cemetery with his throat cut.

On Friday evening an inquest was held on the little girl who was murdered. After some evidence the jury returned a verdict of wilful murder against Abbott.

A LUNATIC IN A RAILWAY TRAIN

On the arrival of the Scotch Mail at Bradford on Tuesday morning, the attention of some of the persons on the platform as the train was drawing up was attracted by the attention of a third-class carriage. Upon a close examination being made a very shocking spectacle presented itself. On opening the door of the compartment two men were discovered covered with blood, the features of one being perfectly unrecognisable. The floor and seats of the carriage had the look of a slaughterhouse. The two men, when the train stopped, were found in a standing position tightly grasping each other. One appeared to be a gentleman in a good position of life, being well dressed and wearing a considerable quantity of jewellery; the other person was so covered with blood that his features could not be recognised, but seemed by his clothing to belong to the artisan class. The latter was found upon the arrival of the doctor to be dead.

It appears that the deceased man, who was being conveyed to London by a Sheriff's officer, under a warrant from the Lord Provost of Glasgow, took out a razor from his pocket and attempted to murder the officer by aiming a blow at his throat. The officer avoided the blow but received a small cut on his ear and left hand and tried to take the razor from his antagonist, who, finding his efforts foiled, drew the razor across his own throat, inflicting a tremendous gash and nearly severing the head from the body.

An inquest was held on the body of the deceased in the afternoon and the evidence given showed that he was subject to epileptic fits, and the jury returned a verdict of suicide while in an unsound state of mind.

MURDEROUS ATTACK BY A GORILLA

A brief report has reached us of a fearful adventure at Famber. It appears that Madame Cartinet and her sister Mdlle Proche, wife and sister in law of an African merchant, have been residing at the above named place for some weeks past. M. Cartinet was always away in the day-time and indeed for some days in succession. Mdlle Proche and her sister occupied the same sleeping apartment during the absence of the latter's husband and had just finished their toilettes when the window of the room was flung open to admit a monstrous gorilla. **The hideous monster rummaged through the drawers and eventually laid hold of** a razor which he flourished and chattered in evident delight. He sprang suddenly forward and attacked Mdlle Proche, the poor lady struggling to free herself from her assailant. The gorilla inflicted severe wounds on the throat and neck of his victim who had by this time fainted from loss of blood.

MURDEROUS ATTACK BY A GORILLA

A gentleman, a soldier, went to the assistance of the two ladies, having been aroused by the piercing screams of both ladies. Upon arriving at the scene the terrible situation of the inmates of the room became apparent. The soldier levelled his revolver and fired three shots in rapid succession. The gorilla fell at the third shot and died some few hours afterwards. The ladies wounds were treated and it is hoped they will not prove fatal, This, however, it is not possible to tell at present.

FORTUNE TELLING AT ROTHERHAM

Jane Woodhead of Parkgate, was charged with Fortune Telling. On the 1st inst, Police Constable Snowden and a man named Amos Gamble went to the defendant's house and requested to be told their fortunes. She produced a pack of cards and shuffled them. Snowden and his companion then shuffled the cards and cut them in three. The defendant then took them up, examined them, and asked Snowden if the party he was after was anything like her. She also told him that he was going to have a light haired young woman and that he would have some money left to him. Defendant said she had people coming to her five times a week from the district around. She said she told a lady that her husband would never eat another Christmas dinner with her, and he died in a fortnight. She charged them 6d. each.

Defendant was sent to gaol for ten days.

AN ENCOUNTER WITH A MAD DOG AT A POST OFFICE

On Tuesday last week at about half past eleven, a large dog, in a rabid state, ran into the General Post Office and caused great excitement among the officials. Luckily he was caught in the door by the foot and detained until the arrival of two police constables and a fireman, who speedily despatched the poor creature. We may add that the dog flew at several persons in Cheapside before it arrived at the Post Office. A crowd of at least two hundred persons had collected around the last named place before the animal was killed.

SUICIDE ON A RAILWAY
A Young Woman Decapitated

An inquest has been held at Reading on the body of a young married woman. It appeared from the statement of the witnesses that the deceased was so ill-treated by her husband in a drunken fit, that in her frenzied state she abandoned her two young children and fled from her home. It would also seem that she must have deliberately laid down on the line for a train to pass over her. The jury returned a verdict that the deceased committed suicide while labouring under a fit of insanity, brought on by the ill-treatment of her husband.

AN EXTRAORDINARY SUICIDE

The LAFAYETTE JOURNAL reports an extraordinary case of suicide committed by James A. Moon, a farmer in good circumstances, residing about nine miles away from that city. He engaged a room at the "Lahr House" Hotel, and on the following day it was found that he had erected in it a guillotine constructed by himself, by which he had been decapitated. Where the cord connected with the axe was fastened, it was divided and a candle inserted between the strands, so that when the candle burned down sufficiently, the two strands would come together and the cord would be burned in two. Right under where the axe would fall a

soap box was secured, screwed to the wall and floor, with the opening outward into the room, so arranged that the axe could come done in front of the box, the upper edges being bevelled to secure a straight stroke from the implement. The axe, the irons in which it was clamped, and the timbers in the beam, altogether weighed a hundred or more pounds, to say nothing of the force of the fall, a distance of six feet.

After arranging the machine the suicide appeared to have laid down on the floor at right angles with the guillotine, buckled a strap which was screwed down to the floor, around his thighs, buckled another around

his body, which was similarly fastened to the floor, put both his hands inside his suspenders lying of course upon his back, and placed his head inside the box above mentioned. The box was filled with cotton wadding saturated with chloroform. To keep the chin out of the way holes were made in each side of the box and a wooden rod ran through upon which the chin rested. It is supposed that having the machinery arranged to his satisfaction, the suicide laid himself upon the floor, arranged the straps, applied the chloroform to the cotton, placed his head in the box, and calmly slept until the axe descended. **When the candle was burned down sufficiently the cord was burned off and the axe fell, completely severing** the head from the body. The head remained in the box while the blood flowed out upon the floor and accumulated in a great pool.

DISASTROUS FLOODS

Terrible Scene

An eye witness described some terrible scenes at the recent floods in the neighbourhood of Green Mountains. The Otter Creek and Moile became swollen with an influx of water. The overflow from these two streams was pretty astounding; stacks, barns, farm buildings, were carried away, when, to crown all, the village became submerged. The disastrous nature of the inundation, together with the numerous touching incidents described by our correspondent, would occupy more space than we could afford. The one, however, which the reader will find illustrated on our front page cannot be passed over. It appears that the village fled before the advancing water; nevertheless, many met with a watery grave.

A young wife with two of her own children, in addition to some of her

BRUTAL MURDER NEAR CROOK

On the evening of Tuesday last week a most brutal murder was perpetrated at Roddymoor by a man of the name of John Richardson, recently a soldier, on his daughter, a little girl between three and four years of age.

It appears that the perpetrator of the brutal deed cohabited with a woman named Walton (the child's mother), and on the above evening they had been quarrelling, when he kicked the child. He then took her up by the feet, and after swinging her round, tossed her to the end of the room, and finished the deadly work by striking the poor little child between the eyes with his fist. The child soon died from the effects of the brutal treatment.

Duel with Pistols

The custom of duelling has not fallen into disuse on the Continent and other places. This is evidenced by the fact of more than one hostile meeting within the last fortnight. A duel with pistols took place in France between two journalists, in which one was mortally wounded.

DISASTROUS FLOODS. TERRIBLE SCENE

neighbours, was overtaken by the flood, despite the efforts of herself and her companions. The water gained upon them and, encumbered as they were with their wet garments, they became so exhausted that death seemed inevitable. Happily, however, they were cheered up by a working man who was perched on a jutting piece of land. This worthy fellow, perceiving their situation, beseeched the woman to bear up as best she could, and make for a mound or hillock that afforded the best shelter. His advice was followed and eventually the mother and children, not forgetting a black dog, were hauled up to a place of safety.

Fearful death of three children

A fatal accident occurred last week within a short distance of Monmouth. Three boys, two of whom were brothers, climbed up the heights to obtain possession of a bird's nest. When close to the subject of their search a large piece of the earth upon which they had been standing gave way, and the poor little fellows were precipitated into the abyss below. When discovered they were all three dead.

MADNESS AND MURDER
A child drowned by its mother

An inquest was held at Wickham Market in Suffolk, on Tuesday respecting the death of a child aged two years and two months. The deceased was the son of a young woman, named Clara Coleman, who had been confined in the Melton Lunatic Asylum, but was discharged thence in Autumn last, although not cured. Since that time she has resided at her mother's house, and has been watched with great care. On Sunday evening, about seven o'clock, she took the child with her into the yard at the back of the house; and as some time passed without her returning, her parents went to seek her. They were astonished to find that she managed to escape from the yard, and had taken the child with her. About an hour later she returned to the house but did not bring the child. She was in a most pitiable state. Her clothes were completely saturated with water,

and in her hair stuck briars and brambles. There was an unusually wild look about her face, and in her excitement she repeated the words "The bridge, the bridge" but nothing more. A search was made for the child and about ten o'clock the same night its body was found floating in the river nearly two miles away from the house. It seemed clear that the poor mother had in her insanity taken the child with her from the yard, through field after field, bedraggling herself with dirt and wet and catching bits of briar and bramble in her hair, until she reached the riverside. Then she appears to have thrown the child into the water, and so drowned it. How she managed to keep the child quiet throughout the stolen journey cannot be surmised. The jury returned a verdict of "Wilful murder" against the mother.

EXCITING SCENE

Last week a scene of an exciting nature took place in Stepney. An ox that was being driven through the public streets suddenly became restive, and charged several persons, happily without doing any serious injury. It was not until a rope had been thrown over its horns that all danger had passed away.

Fatal Accident to a Signalman

A fatal accident occurred to a signalman on the railway last week within a short distance of Newport. The poor fellow with a companion was engaged in repairing the ironwork. One of the rails supporting this gave way, and the unfortunate man fell headlong on to the line. He was senseless when picked up and died about three hours after the accident.

FATAL ENCOUNTER WITH A SHARK

Mr. James Hatchett of Newbury has forwarded us a letter from his nephew (Mr. Walter Bryant) in which the writer gives a brief but graphic account of an encounter with a shark. We quote therefrom the following passage :—

"This day will not be easily forgotten by me. Indeed it cannot fail to be remembered with mournful associations by all on board our little craft.

We were near the coast of Newfoundland when a sudden cry came from all hands on deck: 'a man overboard!' I immediately rushed aft and beheld Joseph Woodward (the young man who danced with Annie the whole evening at the Assembly Rooms) swimming manfully for his life in the wake of our vessel. I shouted out to him as loud as my lungs would permit, to be of good cheer. We slackened sail and tacked about, and in a few moments I had the satisfaction (vain and transitory as this afterwards proved to be) of beholding Joe within a short distance of the vessel's side. A rope was thrown to him by our boatswain. A horrible cry of anguish and despair reached our ears. I saw (oh! my dear uncle may you never behold such a sight) poor Joe Woodward literally snapped in two by the jaws of a monstrous shark. For pity's sake do not make Annie acquainted with his sad fate; leave it to me to break it to her gently. A white lie in this case is pardonable".

Cat's meat man attacked by dogs

On Friday last week, within a mile or so of Middleton, an itinerant purveyor of meat to dogs and cats, was going his usual rounds, when to his infinite surprise and alarm, a pack of hounds rushed at his barrow and the basket he carried, and proceeded to devour the food so ravenously that the poor cat's meat man began to think that he was himself destined to fall a victim to his voracious assailants. Resistance being out of the question he therefore let the animals eat up the dainty viands without attempting to offer

BRUTAL TREATMENT OF A CAT AT HUDDERSFIELD

BRUTAL TREATMENT OF A CAT

On Monday, Patrick Glynn, a labourer was charged at Huddersfield with cruelty to a cat. The defendant had seized the cat by the hind legs, dashed its head against a tub, wrapped it round his arms until the skin and hair came from the body and forced its eyes out. The prisoner who appeared to be labouring under some delusion stated that he had been haunted by the cat for five years and it was better that he should kill it than it should "cut his throat". He was committed to prison for two months.

any opposition.

The keeper of the dogs eventually arrived with a heavy whip and managed to keep them in subjection while he fed them with meat from the barrow. It transpired that the dogs had been a long time without food and the gate of the yard in which they were kept had been accidentally left open, and hence it was that they rushed out and made an onslaught on the cat's meat man.

DEATH FROM SWALLOWING A MOUSE

A most extraordinary occurrence was brought to light a few days ago at an inquest held on the body of a man in South London. From the evidence it appears that in a workroom where many young girls were at work, a mouse suddenly made its appearance on a table, causing, of course, considerable commotion. The intruder was seized, however, by a young man who happened to be present, but the mouse slipped out of his hand and running up his sleeve, came out between his waistcoat and shirt at the neck. **The unfortunate man had his mouth open and the mouse darted thither, and in his fright and surprise the man actually swallowed it. That a mouse can exist for a considerable time without much air has long been a popular belief, and was unfortunately proved to be a fact in the present instance, for the mouse began to tear and gnaw inside the man's throat and chest and the unfortunate fellow died after a little while in the most horrible agony.** Several witnesses having corroborated the above facts and medical evidence having been given as to the cause of death, a verdict of accidental death was returned. The mouse has been preserved in spirits of wine and has been placed in the museum of a London Hospital.

THE EXECUTION OF HOEDEL

Berlin was startled by the sudden, though not unexpected announcement of the extreme penalty of the law having been inflicted on Hoedel for his attempt on the Emperor's life. Preparations for the last act of the terrible drama, which had been carried out most secretly, as since 1866, when the Emperor confirmed for the last time a death warrant, no executions have taken place in

DEATH FROM SWALLOWING A MOUSE

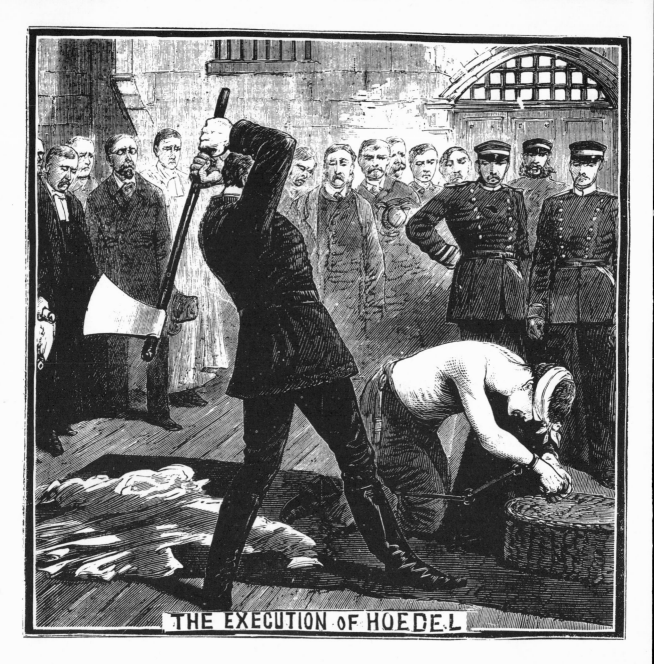

THE EXECUTION OF HOEDEL

Prussia, the instruments necessary for the decapitation had to be borrowed from the Museum, where they had been exposed to public view. Notwithstanding the publication of the news at the beginning of the week, no one believed that Hoedel's end was really so near at hand.

On Thursday morning Hoedel was officially acquainted with the contents of the Crown Prince's order. He remained perfectly quiet, the only sign of inward emotion being the spread of a deadly pallor over his face. Being questioned as to his last wishes, he requested to be executed in public and asked for cigars, some beer and paper to write a letter.

Punctually, at six o'clock in the morning, Hoedel was led to the scaffold temporarily erected in the prison yard. Hoedel, followed by the warders was dressed in the costume worn by him on the day of the attempted assassination. At the urgent request of the clergyman who was walking by his side, Hoedel on leaving his cell threw away the cigar stump, which he had intended to smoke to the very last. At this moment the bell tolled out its dire tones. The executioner who had been quietly standing holding the axe behind him, then advanced, and with one powerful stroke that cut the air like lightning, severed the head from the body.

AN INHUMAN FATHER

At the Nottingham Town Hall on Friday a man named Joseph Foster, who was dressed as a labourer, was charged with a cruel assault upon his child, a boy eleven years of age. It appears that a few nights before the prisoner went home in a drunken state, picked up the child and deliberately threw him on a large fire which was burning in the house at the time. Fortunately he was rescued by a neighbour before he was seriously hurt. The Bench sent Foster to gaol for a month.

Dreadful child murder at Hull

On Thursday morning last week a murder was committed at Hull by a woman named Jane Crompton, the sufferer being her own child, Sarah Alice, a girl a few months old whose head the wretched parent had severed from the body. About eight o'clock in the morning, the prisoner's husband, who is a baker, left his home in Osborne Street, his wife and children then being in the house all right. Shortly after he had gone, his wife called in a neighbour, who looked on the bed and saw the body of the child with its head cut off. Information was at once given to the police and Police-constable Dixey went to the house and took the mother into custody. On charging her with the murder she replied "Yes, I have done it." In the room a new knife was found which had slight stains of blood on it. The weapon appeared to have been cleaned after it had been used.

The father of the deceased identified the body. He had been married for two years and had two children. The one living was called Bertha Ann three years of age. His wife, who was thirty years of age, had wandered in her mind strangely during the past few weeks. She had told a neighbour that she could not do well to the child. She had no milk the child being fed by a bottle. When he left home in the morning, his wife who appeared to be in good spirits, was up and dressed. Deceased was on her knee and the eldest child was getting her breakfast. To the best of his knowledge she was very fond of the child although she said it was a deal of trouble with the bottle. His wife never took much drink and he was certain she had nothing to drink that morning.

A neighbour, Mrs. Alice Fox, said she noticed Mrs. Crompton appeared to have taken a dislike to her child. She had on one occasion told witness she would be doing something to the child, and from that time witness had become very suspicious and often visited Mrs. Crompton. She idolised her elder daughter Bertha. A short time after eight that morning Mrs. Crompton walked into witness's room. She said "Mrs. Fox will you go into my room?" Witness asked "What for?" she replied "I have done something to Sarah Alice. I have cut her head off." Witness rushed into the room leaving the mother sitting in an arm chair. On getting into the room she saw the child with its head off.

Police-constable Dixey deposed to being directed to the house. On going upstairs he saw the body with the head some distance from it. He said to the prisoner "I charge you with the murder of your child". She replied "Yes, I have." She got her shawl and he took her away as the neighbours were getting excited. She stated she would never have done this had two women who lived next door treated her as they ought, so she took her revenge on her baby. She sometimes thought she would drown both her children.

The Coroner then summed up; the jury at once found a verdict of "Wilful Murder" against Jane Crompton.

ATTEMPT TO DROWN A SUPPOSED WITCH

On Thursday, last week, an old woman named Margaret Grover, or "Peg" Grover as she is more familiarly termed, was most cruelly treated by some of the rustic population, within a few miles of the town of Newport. It appears that for some long time past the more superstitious have been under the impress-ion that poor "Peg" was a witch; this impression seemed to gain strength as time went on, and every description of misfortune that befell the village, was laid at the door of the old woman. In the early part of last week a little girl named Sarah Parvis died somewhat suddenly. Her death was attributed to the wicked machin-ation of Peg Grover who, unfortun-ately, chanced to be in the neigh-bourhood at the time. Some working men, who implicitly believed in the story of witchcraft, seized hold of "Peg", passed a rope round her waist, and threw her into the water, the rope was then drawn over the branch of a tree, and the poor old

ATTEMPT TO DROWN A SUPPOSED WITCH

woman was hauled up for a moment and then again immersed. This process was repeated ten or a dozen times at the very least, to the infinite amusement of the bystanders, and the probability is that it would have ended in the death of the old woman, had it not been for the intervention of one or two of the neighbouring residents, who came to her rescue and released her from the hands of her tormentors.

CRUEL TREATMENT OF AN ORPHAN

At Norwich, Mrs. Savage, the wife of a tradesman living in the city, was charged with cruelly ill-treating Rose Hall, an orphan girl, who resided with her as domestic servant. It appeared that the defendant had beaten the poor girl with a brush, a stick and her fists, and had also kicked and jumped upon her while she was sweeping the floors. The magistrates committed the defendant for two months, with three weeks further imprisonment in default of paying costs.

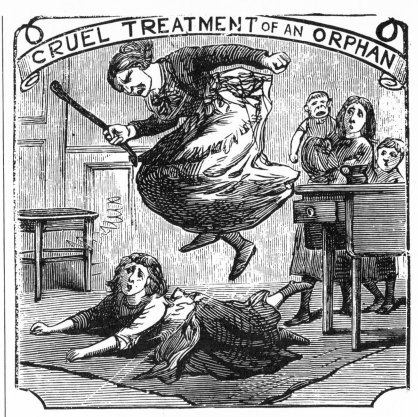

CRUEL TREATMENT OF AN ORPHAN

KILLING A SUPPOSED WITCH

A very singular charge of murder was tried at Warwick Assizes on Wednesday last week, before Baron Bramwell. James Haywood, agricultural labourer, forty years of age, and a Wesleyan, was charged with the wilful murder of Anne Tenant, at Long Compton, Warwickshire. It was proved in evidence that fully one third of the villagers believed in witch craft. The prisoner, believing in the common superstition, stabbed the deceased, who was eighty years of age, with a pitchfork, under the impression that she was one of the fifteen witches he ought to kill. It was admitted that on all other subjects he was sane. He justified his conduct by referring to verses from Leviticus:— "A man also or woman that hath a familiar spirit, or that is a wizard, should be put to death; they shall stone them with stones; their blood shall be upon them." The judge said that such a prevalence of this superstition would be disgraceful to savages. The prisoner was found to have been insane at the time, and was ordered to be kept in confinement during Her Majesty's pleasure.

KILLING A SUPPOSED WITCH

A HORRIBLE TALE OF THE SEA
A Skeleton Crew

The schooner Lancaster, whilst bound to Sydney, from Charlestown, Prince Edward's Island, on the 18th August, fell in with a dismasted vessel, which was apparently deserted. The Captain of the Lancaster, with several of his crew, saw on boarding the wreck, which we . extract from the MORNING ADVERTISER.

"Splintered spars, entangled in canvas and rigging gear, and the planks of a boat torn asunder by wind and sea. More dismal still were the scenes which further investigation brought to light. Below a heap of motley rigging and broken by the weight of a spar which lay across it, were the bones of a human being—a skeleton. The skull and ribs had been crushed almost on a level with the deck. Shreds of canvas trousers and a guernsey frock were found among and near the bones. Further search revealed five other skeletons. A slight covering of crisped flesh lay on four of the skeletons, showing they had died more recently than the other two. Many of the utensils of the galley were found and Captain Martin made a search among them to assure himself whether there had been any food on board at the time of the death of these men. Not a single remaining pot or vessel in the cooking department contained the least particle of food. This appeared to satisfy the Captain that all on board had perished from hunger. The spectacle on board the dreary sepulchral hull was at least appalling. It was ascertained that the vessel had

A HORRIBLE TALE OF THE

been rigged a brig. The hull bore no name but on the bowsprit the word "Glenalvon" was barely legible.

The wheelhouse had been broken away and the fastening of the rudder broken. This, as the Captain remarked, was the work of some tremendous sea. The foremast had been cut away to save the vessel from foundering—one of the extremest emergencies in a hurricane at sea.

Entering the cabin a foul odour was discovered, but not intense enough to forbid a thorough investigation. Towards the end of the steps leading down to the cabin a foetid pool of water was seen and the men had to wade through it to reach every portion of the cabin. Between a stationary table and a couch the head of a corpse protruded from a berth in the wall and when brought on deck it was found to be in a state of decay. A buttoned jacket of good material, blue pantaloons, a flannel shirt marked 'T.T.' and one boot covered the corpse. The chronometer in the cabin pointed to halfpast four o'clock, and on the table was an open Bible turned downward, a revolver with two chambers loaded, and a bottle containing a piece of paper upon which was written 'Jesus guide this to some helper. Merciful God don't let us perish'.

In the Captain's state room his corpse was found lying bent on the floor, as though he had fallen from weakness, while struggling with faint hope to save himself and men. On his bed were scattered books, papers etc. one sheet of which attracted peculiar attention being a letter to his wife assuring her of his well-being.

The ship's regular papers were not found open but Captain Martin took charge of a neat writing desk found in the Captain's trunk and locked.

At seven o'clock in the evening Captain Martin performed the sorrowful services of a burial at sea. For coffins a quantity of old canvas was used and rude bags were quickly formed of that material. The ceremony over the party put back again for the Lancaster, happy to quit the gloomy craft that harboured so many dead, heard so many dying groans and such awful roaring of the wind and sea, that had caused all that death and destruction. Captain Martin has procured every possible clue, all of which he will give to the authorities at Sydney, so that the true history of the Glenalvon may be learned."

A—A SKELETON CREW

ROBBING SCHOOLGIRLS OF THEIR WEARING APPARREL

On Saturday night last some burglars contrived to force an entrance into Miss Parkhouse's establishment for young ladies, which is situated in the immediate vicinity of Hadley. After ransacking the premises below, and transferring to the bag they carried, all the valuables within their reach, they crept into one of the bedrooms in which three young ladies were sleeping. The thieves coolly proceeded to possess themselves of the wearing apparel of the occupants of the chamber. One of the young ladies, a Miss Matilda—was aroused by the movements of the intruders. She opened her eyes, and beheld a masked ruffian by her bedside, who swore he would take her life if she attempted to give an alarm. The poor girl was so paralysed with fear that she found it impossible to give utterance to the faintest sound. The two miscreants succeeded in making good their retreat with a heavy booty.

—•—

LOSS OF A HULL FISHING SMACK

Last week a Hull smack foundered during a gale. An attempt was made by the crew to put off in one of the boats, which however was speedily capsized. The smack together with eight mariners disappeared beneath the surface of the water, and the vessel and all hands were lost.

THE WHITECHAPEL TRAGEDY

The East of London has been startled by its propriety by the discovery of a great crime, which has been the crowning event of the week. Since the murder of Mullins, no event of its kind, has so disturbed the public mind. All the elements of mystery and horror have once more united, to prove truth stranger then fiction, reality greater than romance, stern facts triumphant over the products of imagination. When the blatent rumour spread the story of the discovery, and fed upon the horrible surroundings of the case, enlarged its mystery and sent a thrill of fearful emotion through the community, it was sufficient for all intelligent minds that the recovery of two parcels of mutilated humanity disclosed the evidence of a terrible murder; but when the name of the person upon whom guilty suspicion accumulated became known, it would have been difficult to determine whether dubious astonishment, or unmitigated horror, were in the ascendant.

As may be well imagined the excitement and interest in this case were concentrated in the proceedings at the Southwark Police Court on Tuesday.

The statement that Harry Wainwright, who stands charged with the murder of Harriet Lane, was at one time well known at many of the London Institutes as a lecturer and entertainer, is quite correct. A correspondent, who was acquainted with Wainwright some years since, describes him as being a man of undoubted ability, and certainly remarkable for assurance and self-possession.

At the resumed inquest on Harriet Lane, whose mutilated remains were found in the possession of the man Henry Wainwright, now under remand from the Southwark Police Court upon the charge of murder, the Coroner, upon opening the Court, enquired "What course do you propose to adopt?" The Coroner had understood the jury were anxious to finish the enquiry that night. They had already been taken from their business three times and he did not think it advisable to keep a matter of this kind open too long. It was agreed to adjourn the enquiry and after some discussion October 14th, was fixed upon.

ATTEMPTED MURDER AT HULL

A man named Windross was shot through the head at Hull on Monday, by his brother-in-law and is in a hopeless condition. It appears that Windross and Goodyear, who shot him, have been on unpleasant terms, the latter objecting to interference in family affairs. Windross went to Goodyear's and enquired about Mrs. Goodyear, his sister, and after some words Goodyear deliberately shot over the counter at him. The bullet which was discharged entered his forehead. When arrested Goodyear gave up a new six chambered revolver and a box of cartridges, and admitted his guilt.

THE WHITECHAPEL TRAGEDY

THE FLYING MAN "BAT"
EXTRAORDINARY FEAT OF AN AERONAUT

Mr. Roffley, in his interesting work, entitled "Moving Bodies in the Air", gives an account of an eccentric and enterprising Englishman, called "Bat". This person many years ago made more than one attempt to fly over more than one city on the Continent, and it would appear if we are to accept the authority quoted, that his efforts were attended with some degree of success, for, on one occasion, he succeeded in flying through the air by means of an ingenious apparatus invented by himself, for the space of twenty minutes. The machinery he used was much the same, we suppose, as the recent attempt made by another professor at Brussels. "Bat" ascended by means of a small balloon. Having attained an altitude sufficient for his purpose, he unfolded a pair of wings attached to his legs and arms, by means of which he propelled himself along. The illustration in our front page is copied from an engraving printed in Mr. Roffley's book. "Bat" it appears was overtaken by death before he could bring his invention to perfection.

A paragraph which we quote from a daily paper describes the signal failure of an attempt made by M. Groof a week or so before.

The Flying Man at Brussels

Mr. Groof's attempt on Sunday to fly over Brussels, was an utter fiasco. When only two or three feet from the ground he ignominiously came down, falling on his face. The mob that he gathered grew furious at the disappointment, and tore to pieces the balloon that was to have played a subordinate part in the performance. Stones were thrown about recklessly and a scene of serious disorder was witnessed. A number of ladies were hurt, and the disturbance has resulted in numerous arrests. It is a pity Icarus escaped so well after causing so much mischief.

KILLED BY A BICYCLE

KILLED BY A BICYCLE

On Friday, last week, a sad accident occurred within two or three miles of Newtown. Two bicyclists were going along a narrow lane at full speed, when a woman with a market basket, who was walking towards the lane by a footway leading into it, came in front of the two bicyclists, who strove in vain to come to a halt. A collision was unavoidable; the woman was knocked down by one bicycle, and the other, despite the efforts of the rider, the wheels passed over the legs; and the injuries, although apparently of no very serious nature at first, assumed a grave aspect on the Sunday and Monday after, when the ill-fated woman gradually sank, and expired early on the morning of Wednesday.

THROWING A WIFE OUT OF A WINDOW

William Henry Sands, lodging house keeper, of George Street, Bloomsbury, was charged at Bow Street, on remand, with violently assaulting his wife, and with attempting to throw her out of window. Rose Sands, the wife of the prisoner, whose face was fearfully bruised, stated that she and her husband were very good friends up till two o'clock in the afternoon of the 8th inst. There had, however, been some little jealousy, for she believed him to be paying his addresses to a barmaid, to whom he meant to give a ring. The prisoner later in the day quietly asked her to follow him upstairs. She did so; but when they got into the bedroom he locked the door, put the key in his pocket, and commenced to strike her and kick her. She got under the bed for protection. He, however, lifted up the bed, pulled her out, seized her in his arms and threw her out of the window. It was a first floor window. She caught hold of the ledge with her hands. He then struck her hands, and she fell into the street below.

A little girl, daughter of the prisoner, deposed to seeing her parents fighting, and added that she tried to stop them; and Dr. Ralph, the divisional surgeon, stated that the complainant had been greatly injured by the assault, but not so much by the fall from the window.—The complainant now stated that it was the first time she had ever charged her husband, and begged that the week's imprisonment he had suffered would be deemed sufficient,—Mr. Flowers felt it his duty to sentence the prisoner to six month's hard labour and ordered him to find a surety in £50 and enter into his own recognisances for £100 to keep the peace towards her for twelve months.

AERONAUT ATTACKED BY CROCODILE

The following account of Mr. Lynn's first balloon experience is written by himself, and appears in the Calcutta papers.

"I suppose those who formed the dense concourse in the Northern Circular Road on Saturday, will be interested in reading my description of the voyage, and descent of the balloon. For the purpose of ascertaining my altitude I used an instrument of my own construction; it consists of a small metallic tube, having secured at one end of it and empty, flexible tube of goldbeater's skin.

The view from the altitude of 9,000 feet was sublime beyond description. Every street and garden path was distinctly delineated as upon a coloured map. The Hooghly River appeared like a small silvery snake, and the ships like small black spots upon its back, and whenever I looked westward all the water surfaces seemed to stand up far above the land. The general shout from the vast assemblage on my leaving earth, I distinctly heard a second time after I

had been up fifteen minutes. This was a reverberation. At 4.40 I found I was beginning to move rapidly towards Tiger Point and I was at this moment at an elevation of 13,000 feet. This unpleasant prospect of landing induced me to try and beat a retreat, which I was fortunate enough to accomplish by descending into the current which I found blowing for a few moments from the South East. While now descending, and at an altitude of 10,000 feet in a perfectly clear atmosphere, a vast plain of intense white to the North was open to my view. I cannot form any conception as to the cause of this phenomenon, excepting that the rays of the setting sun had come in contact with a cold blast from the snowy range in the Himalayas. I continued my descent and very soon this phenomenon was lost to me. Although every moment's delay increased my risk in landing, I could not resist the temptation to try and 'fathom' this mystery, but could not succeed.

At 5.15 I was within a thousand feet of terra firma—a rather inappro-

priate name for the locality—when I saw a huge crocodile moving towards me with an impressive steadiness, and when I came down slap into the mud and rushes, which for miles were over 10 feet in height, I saw the monster's head level with the top of the bulrushes. Had there been a slight breeze I think I could have anchored to this brute, fortunately I had enough ballast to throw overboard just as this monster was within fifty yards of me. This enabled me to rise above the thick jungle to the length of my grappling rope— say about 30 feet. I hoped he would soon impale himself upon my grappling iron, but I was doomed to disappointment, for as I had been calling very lustily for help, I found natives wading towards me through the thick mud and rushes.

About half a dozen natives were persuaded by me to puckrao my rope; they led me to believe that they would have been alongside me before but they had seen the crocodile's head near the balloon car. The balloon was wafted over the

AN AERONAUT ATTACKED BY A CROCODILE.

jungle and across creeks for nearly three miles. At last we arrived at a small dry space and here we emptied the balloon and packed it into the car. We had to cross two wide channels; the dead weight was put on the heads of twelve who had the pluck to get across the streams in mud up to their armpits. However, it did not disfigure them as much as I would have been, as they were nude. I was taken across these delectable swizzles on their shoulders. Wat at last arrived with the balloon at the Asiatic Jute Mills at Sourah, and had it not been for the kindness of Mr. Preston and Mr. Miller I am convinced I should never have reached a place of safety. These gentlemen showed me every kindness and here I am safe and sound.''

NOVEL AND FATAL BALLOON DUEL

A deadly encounter between balloonists is reported from Guayana. It appears that M. Molica, a Portuguese gentleman, sent a challenge to a Dutchman, who according to the rules that are adopted in all cases of this sort, had the choice of weapons and manner of meeting. The Dutchman, who is an aeronaut, elected to ascend in his balloon; his adversary to adopt a similar course in a balloon borrowed for the occasion. The terms were agreed to, and each belligerent, accompanied by his second, ascended simultaneously. At a given time the combatants discharged their weapons. M. Molica was wounded slightly, while his antagonist received a mortal wound, from the effects of which he expired in less than two hours. The affair has caused quite a sensation in the locality in which it took place.

FATAL ACCIDENT TO CHILDREN

An accident of a most exciting character took place a few days ago at Vera Cruz. At the end of a fair held in the locality, a balloon was announced to ascend, the aeronauts being Christoph and Andreas Gemara. All the preliminary proceedings went on in a satisfactory way. The balloon was inflated, the brothers Gemara "took their places in the car" and in a few minutes the balloon began to ascend. All of a sudden a piercing scream caused considerable consternation to the spectators. Every eye was turned in the direction from whence the sound proceeded. Two young ladies were suspended beneath the car of the balloon. Their situation was indeed a fearful one.

It appeared, (so we gathered from what afterwards transpired) that one of the ropes attached to the car had dragged along the ground, and eventually wound itself around the body of a young lady named Anna Lingrave, the daughter of an American merchant, and by this she was carried up, Her sister perceiving the dangerous position of Anna, clung to her in the hopes of either staying the course of the balloon or else releasing the tethered young lady. In the space of a few brief seconds, however, both the Misses Lingrave were carried to a fearful height.

Andreas Gemara succeeded in getting hold of the end of the rope which held Anna Lingrave. This he held firmly that there should be no possibility of it becoming uncoiled round the body of its beauteous burden; meanwhile his brother Christoph was mindful of the position of Theresa (the elder Miss Lingrave). He held the young lady firmly by one hand, and strove as best he could by words of encouragement to reassure her, and begged of her not to give way to groundless fears, as all might yet be well. The balloon continued on its silent course over "vine clad" hills and fertile valleys, until eventually Christoph Gemara succeeded in opening the valve. Then after a brief but intense agony of suspense to the four living creatures attached to it, the aerial monster began slowly to descend. Ropes were thrown out from the car, to one of which a grappling iron was attached. In the course of a few minutes the sisters reached terra firma in safety, and were released from their perilous position, but the remembrance of what they had passed through will last them their lives.

Dr. Lankester held an inquest a few days ago at the "Globe Tavern", Derby Street, on Ernest Gregory, aged five, son of a clerk, residing at 44, Milman Street, Grays Inn Road. Deceased and two younger children were playing with a soda water cork and wire, and sitting in infants' chairs placed on a table in front of the first floor front room window, which was open. About eleven inches above the bottom of the sash was a wooden guard to prevent anything falling against the window glass. This guard had been removed by some painters and the mother had to fix it. The children began to quarrel about the cork, and to put a stop to their noise the mother took the cork away and threw it out of the window, and gave her attention to some domestic duty at the other end of the room. The children looked over the guard to see what had become of the cork, when the fastening of the guard suddenly gave way, and deceased fell out of the window into the area below, and was killed on the spot. Just as he fell he clutched hold of the other two children, pulling them out with him; the little girl fell on the body of deceased, and escaped with some severe bruises, and the other a little boy two and half years old, owing to being caught by the door landing, escaped with his life, but now lies in the Royal Free Hospital suffering from some severe fractures. A verdict of "Accidental Death" was returned.

FEARFUL BALLOON ACCIDENT-NARROW ESCAPE

Attempted Suicide
Awful Situation

On Friday afternoon, last week, the inhabitants of the little village of Drysett, in Somersetshire, were witnessed of an appalling scene, which is happily one of rare and exceptional character. A young female was discovered by a policeman hanging head downwards from a window of her father's house. At first the officer concluded that she was dead; a movement of the body and head convinced him that he had come to an erroneous conclusion.

He hastened at once and procured a ladder, when upon his returning to the house in question, he saw the female still in the horrible situation. By this time a host of villagers surrounded the habitation. The policeman assisted by a farm labourer, succeeded in rescuing the young lady from what appeared to be certain death. It was some hours, however, before the latter recovered her consciousness, and she is even at the present time in a very critical situation. It appears from what our reporter has been able to glean, that the lady, whose name is Miss Edith Hugglestone, has been for a long time past subject to terrible delusions. So powerful have these been that her mind became affected, and on Friday she opened one of the windows for the purpose of leaping out of the same to terminate her existence. By a most fortunate circumstance she was saved—both the sash lines of the window were broken, and when the unhappy girl strove to precipitate herself, the window closed with a sudden bang, and caught a portion of her dress and petticoats; thus did she remain suspended until timely succour came.

FATAL ASSAULT ON A WOMAN

On Monday morning last week at the Accrington Police Court, Michael Kennedy an old man, residing at Clayton, was charged with killing Deborah Dowd, wife of John Dowd, labourer of the same place. On Sunday night the prisoner went into Dowd's house drunk, seized a chair and struck Mrs. Dowd a blow on the head fracturing her skull. She died in three quarters of an hour. The prisoner was remanded until Thursday to await the Coroner's inquest.

PLAYING AT WAINWRIGHT

Two remarkably narrow escapes from hanging are reported.

On Tuesday last a rather ludicrous but what might have proved a fatal case of hanging occurred at Bedworth. A number of youths joined in a game called "Wainwright" and for that purpose drew cuts for the characters represented by the late tragedy. After a trial of three hours duration, the one whose part it was to enact Wainwright was found guilty and sentenced to be hanged. The youth who represented Marwood was compelled to pinion the prisoner who was then marched to a place of execution. Arrived at the spot they took leather belts from their waists, fastened them together and placed a noose round his neck. He was then hoisted on the shoulders of Marwood and the other end of the strap was fastened to the iron projecting from the lamp-post. The executioner was then forced to loose his charge and they ran off, leaving him, as they thought, hanging to the lamp-post. Fortunately the strap gave way at the buckle so what might have been tragic terminated as a farce.

PLAYING AT WAINWRIGHT

SUICIDE OF A BUTCHER'S WIFE AT BOLTON

On Thursday, last week, Mr. Taylor, Borough Coroner held an inquest on Catherine Ann Kinch, aged 31, wife of a Butcher, William Kinch. Kinch who was first to give evidence stated that on Monday morning deceased came to the market hall and some words passed between them. Deceased told witness he was not fit to go to the Manchester market to buy beasts. She then went to the King's Arms and bought two beasts there. Witness never saw deceased again as he went and stayed all night at the house of his brother-in-law.

Thomas Collier, having missed deceased, decided he would call at the house. He found the front door open but no sign of her and shouting, but receiving no answer, subsequently proceeded to the cellar of the house **where he found deceased hanging with a rope round her neck.** Witness was so terrified he ran away to get assistance. The woman seemed to be quite dead. The jury thought she hung herself under temporary derangement and returned a verdict accordingly.

SUICIDE OF A BUTCHER'S WIFE AT BOLTON

FATAL CASE OF ELEPHANT TEASING

On Wednesday, last week, at Newcastle, Staffordshire, Mr. J. Knight, Borough Coroner, held an inquest on the body of George Stanton, the boy who died from injuries inflicted upon him at Hanley, by an elephant belonging to Messrs. Bostock and Wombwell's menagerie. Mr. John Jones, of the Talbot Inn, Hanley. stated that on Saturday morning he saw a number of children round an elephant in a passage leading to the Angel Inn. The children were feeding the animal with nuts and bread. After looking on for a few minutes, he turned to go away, but hearing the children cry he went back, and saw the elephant holding a boy against a wall. The keeper was seven or eight yards away and he shouted, upon which the elephant let the boy drop and directly afterwards he was carried away. Witness heard one of the children say that the boy who had been hurt had given the elephant a stone.

Samuel Carr, the ostler at the Angel Inn, stated that the elephant had been brought to his master's premises, and was standing in the yard while he went to fetch the key of the stable. When he came with the key he saw the animal "squeezing" the boy against the wall. It then took the lad with its trunk, and the keeper shouting at it, it threw the lad against the wall. He was sure it took the lad up with its trunk. The keeper was six or seven yards away from the elephant. Thomas Birch, potter, said that he saw some children playing with the elephant, and he told them it would hurt them if they teased it. He saw the elephant push one of the boys down and lift him with its trunk but dropped him again when the keeper shouted.

Jesse Stanton, cratemaker, Newcastle, the father of the deceased, stated that he fetched his son home on the Saturday. He was injured at the back of the head and his back was scarred. He said that the elephant had "squeezed" him against the wall. He died on Sunday evening.

Thomas Hurley said he was elephant keeper in the employ of Messrs. Bostock and Wombwell. He was with the elephant at Hanley on Saturday, at the Angel. While waiting for the key of the stable, he stood about two yards from the elephant, which was being fed by a number of children. He had driven the children away several times, but they returned. He saw the elephant pushing the boy against the wall with its trunk, he shouted and the elephant turned away. The boy was then removed. The elephant was a female about twelve years of age and was usually very quiet and harmless. It had never injured anyone before.

The jury returned a verdict that the boy died from having been crushed by an elephant.

FATAL CASE OF ELEPHANT TEASING

FEARFUL ENCOUNTER.

FEARFUL ENCOUNTER WITH A BOA CONSTRICTOR

A very terrible story reaches us from Texas. A lady, the wife of a merchant named Wilkinson, was, while on the borders of a forest, attacked by a huge boa constrictor, which wound itself around her body, evidently with the intention of crushing her to death. Mr. Wilkinson was aroused by his wife's piercing shrieks, and hastened at once to the spot. Happily, he did not lose his presence of mind, and he at once proceeded to attack the hideous reptile. At such a time moments seem ages. Mr. Wilkinson severed the head of the reptile from its body, besides inflicting other injuries. Mrs. Wilkinson, during this double encounter became insensible, and it is anticipated that the shock to the system is of so serious a nature that a long time must necessarily elapse before she can hope to recover from the effects of the trial she has undergone.

ATTACKED BY LIONS

Mr. Jamrach's museum and collection of birds and other natural curiosities, in Ratcliff Highway, is so well known, that it would be a work of superogation to offer any prolix comments upon its many and varied points of interest. The museum itself is well worthy of a visit and the ornithological specimens in the adjoining shop are equally rare and curious. Two turnings eastward beyond the last-named establishment is a menagerie, and we are able to testify from ocular demonstration to the attractive nature of this; indeed, we do not remember ever having seen a finer collection of wild beasts in any private collection. The three noble lions in the cage at the end of entrance yard are magnificent specimens. The attack made upon a man by these terrific-looking creatures, forms the subject of one of our illustrations in this week's number.

It appears that a few days ago a working man was lifting an empty case on to another, and while so engaged he stood close to the bars of the den containing the lions, who

53

seized hold of him with their formidable claws. His cries attracted the attention of an attendant who ran to his assistance, but upon finding himself attacked by the fierce brutes he hastily retreated. Another person in Mr. Jamrach's employ hastened to the spot, and with great courage and presence of mind, which cannot be too highly commended, succeeded in dragging the unfortunate man from the lion's grasp, not however, before very serious injuries had been sustained. It was at first thought that the wounds would prove fatal.

The accident is attributed to an act of carelessness on part of the injured man, who, heedless of danger, imprudently chose to place himself within reach of those voracious beasts of prey. It is but justice to the owner of the menagerie in question to note that he is especially mindful of those in his employ, and the healthy appearance of the animals themselves prove most incontestibly the care that is bestowed upon them.

APPALLING SCENE
THE CROCODILE AND ITS PREY

A correspondent of the Delhi Gazette relates a terrible scene which occurred the other day at Etawah, at the funeral ceremonies of a native. The corpse was brought to the banks of the Jumna to undergo the usual ceremony of burning. It was laid on the sand about fifteen yards from the water, while the men were preparing and stacking the wood. This done the wood was fired so as to give some little time for a good blaze, and the men moved off to a little distance, squatting themselves down to have a smoke, when a huge crocodile, seemingly watching their movements, rushed out of the water, seized the corpse and doubled back, making a tremendous header into the river, with the body between his jaws, leaving the followers and mourners in perfect bewilderment.

ATTACKED BY LIONS IN JAMRACK'S MENAGERIE

NARROW ESCAPE
OF A LILLIPUTIAN
TIGER TAMER
VERSUS CATS

From Paris the other day came a story, half grotesque and half revolting, of a cruelly ingenious showman to whom there had occurred the idea of getting up a Lilliputian exhibition of tiger-taming. He procured four cats, whose bodies he painted orange-tawny, with black stripes, so as to be closely imitative of the hide of a felis tigris, and then he engaged a little boy, who, clad in tights and spangles, was to enact the part of a beast tamer, but who, prior to his appearance in public, was shut up in a cage with the cats and instructed to reduce them to subjection, and to teach them a variety of tricks by means of rigorous chastisement. If, however, the poor little tiger king was provided with a switch, the four Lilliputian tigers had been endowed by nature with a due complement of claws; and they so worried and tore the unfortunate lad that, had he not been able to make his escape from the cage, fatal results may have followed. He ran shrieking into the street pursued by his master; but the Police interfered and the Correctional Tribunal may possibly have something very serious to say to the barbarous promoter of Lilliputian tiger-taming exhibitions.

Scarcely, however, has the echo of this affair died away ere we hear of two very alarming accidents which

have occurred to a pair of wild beast tamers in France. At Havre, the lion king, Bidel, has had a sufficiently narrow escape from a horrible death. It was this performer's custom to go into the cage with the wild beasts, bearing with him a sheep which, through the awe inspired by his presence, was kept free from molestation on the part of the ferocious inmates of the den. Recently he entered the cage and placed the sheep on the back of the lioness— a feat which he had often before accomplished with safety. No sooner had he done this, however, than a huge lion sprang upon the unfortunate sheep, burying his teeth in its body. There was commotion and panic among the crowded audience, but the undaunted Bidel stepped forward, and with a heavy bludgeon dealt Leo such a tremendous blow over the jaws, that the beast uttering a yell of pain, was completely cowed, abandoned his bleeding victim and crouched humbly at the feet of his master. The sight and smell of the blood of the sheep were, however, too much for wild beast nature to bear.

The other denizens of the cage began to howl in an ominous manner and with singular unanimity of teeth and claws, they attacked Monsieur Bidel, even as Mr. William Nye went to the Heathen Chinee. The beast tamer, not a whit terrified, chased the first lion into another cage, fought his way back through the remaining brutes and, rescuing his wounded sheep, issued from the den.

GIRL SEIZED BY A GORRILLA

A GIRL SEIZED BY A GORILLA

We have received a sketch, together with a short report, of an incident which occurred a short time ago in Western Africa. The engraving is taken from the sketch forwarded to us by our correspondent who gives the following account:

"Mr. and Mrs. Osgood, a Canadian merchant and his wife, have been travelling through several parts of Western Africa. Mr. Osgood had betaken himself to the woods, accompanied by a guide and native servant, his object being to shoot wild fowl. His wife and daughter were left on a spot upon which the party had encamped some hours previously. While Mrs. Osgood was engaged in domestic duties, her little girl Clara, who was chasing butterflies, **uttered a loud scream and her mother was horrified at seeing her clasped in the arms of a monstrous gorilla who was about to bear her off.** The unhappy lady was perfectly frantic and luckily her husband, who was not far distant, was attracted to the spot by her cries. One barrel of his gun was loaded, he took steady aim, and the whole charge of shot entered the back and posterior of the gorilla, who dropped the child and scampered off, howling with pain.

CHILD STEALING EXTRAORDINARY.

CHILD STEALING EXTRAORDINARY

A thrilling incident took place at Texas, on Wednesday, last week. The facts of the case to which it is more especially connected are of a nature both painful and affecting. It appears that an English lady, who had settled out there some years ago, was given in marriage by her only surviving parent to a Portuguese merchant, named Narildo. For the first few months after the nuptials all went on as merry as a marriage bell. A child was born (a little girl). Mr. Narildo's business called him a great deal away from home. As time went on his journeys were longer and more frequent. His young English wife learned soon after this that her husband had a mistress and a young family at a distant part of the country; when remonstrated with by his wife he did not attempt to deny it. After this the daily life of both husband and wife was embittered by frequent quarrels, the end of this being a mutual agreement for a separation.

Three years passed during which time Narildo saw nothing of his English wife and child, but his love for the former had flown, it was succeeded by a deadly hate. He now determined on taking the child from her. He sent a friend, who informed the unhappy mother, that the father desired her to give up the child. This she positively refused to do and the messenger took his departure. For some months after this his wife was suffered to remain without further threats.

On Wednesday, last week, however, a blow fell upon her, which, it is feared, she will not be able to sustain. While seated in her parlour reading—her daughter meanwhile playing in the room—a rough looking man suddenly leapt through the open window and seized hold of Clarissa, the little girl. The latter screamed loudly for assistance. The mother rushed forward to gain possession of her darling, whereupon another ruffian presented a pistol to her head,

swearing that he would fire if she made any resistance or further outcry. Mrs. Narildo fainted. When she regained her consciousness she found herself on the couch, with a doctor by her side, and her servants in close attendance on her. Clarissa and the two ruffians were gone.

FOUND
DEAD
IN STREETS

Dr. Langham received information of a strange discovery and an unaccountable death of a woman who is supposed to be named Louisa Lorraine, aged 33, but whose address is not known. She was found quite dead lying on the pavement outside Vine Street Police Station by a Police Constable. The acting Inspector had the corpse conveyed to the Mount Street dead-house. The deceased was very stylishly dressed and the feasible conjecture is that she was one of the gay women who frequent the neighbourhood.

ATTEMPTED
MURDER
ON
THE THAMES

On Saturday morning last week at Ilford, Essex, Thomas Simmonds, labourer, was charged with attempting to murder William Munday aged eighteen. It was elicited that the prosecutor and a companion were rowing down the Thames when the prisoner got into the boat and attempted to sink it. Munday prevented him from doing so when he suddenly drew a knife and plunged it into the prosecutor's left side. The prisoner was formally committed for trial. Munday remains under hospital treatment.

BARBAROUS MURDER ALTON, HAMPSHIRE

The usual quiet town of Alton, Hampshire, was on Saturday evening drawn into a state of intense excitement owing to a report being current that a horrid murder had been committed on a child named Fanny Adams, between seven and eight years of age. The rumour, on enquiry, unhappily turned out to be too true.

From particulars obtained and which can be relied on, it seems that three children, the deceased Fanny Adams, her younger sister and a girl named Warner about the same age as the deceased, of respectable parents residing in Tan-House Lane, Alton, were playing in Flood Meadow at the back of Mr. Jefferie's tan yard, distance from their residence about 400 yards, when they were accosted between one and two o'clock in the

afternoon by a Mr. Frederick Baker, a young man of great respectability, clerk to Messrs. Clement & Son, Solicitors, of that town. It appears that Baker offered deceased a halfpenny to go with him up a hollow, or old road, leading to the village of Shelton, by the side of a hop garden belonging to Messrs. Henry and John Chalcraft, farmers, and Warner three halfpence to take the sister away and not to come with him and the deceased. Fanny took the halfpenny but declined going with him to the place mentioned, whereupon Baker took hold of her hand and led her away crying. The two girls left wandered about the fields until about five o'clock in the evening when they returned home.

A Mrs. Gardiner residing in the locality saw them return without Fanny and wished to know where the deceased was. Warner replied that she was gone with Baker up the hollow mentioned. Mrs. Gardiner communicated with the mother of the deceased what the children had told her concerning Fanny and they started together to search for the missing child. After proceeding they met Baker returning to the town, close by a gate which separates the hop garden from the meadow. Mrs. Gardiner enquired of Baker what he had done with the child to which he replied "Nothing". She then said did you give Warner threehalfpence to return and leave you with Fanny—at least she has told us so? The prisoner then said "No I did not. I gave her threepence to buy some sweets which I often do to children". Mrs. Gardiner observed I have a great mind to give you in charge of the Police. Baker rejoined she might do as she liked. The quiet way in which he answered combined with the respectable position occupied by the prisoner, at once threw off any suspicion which might have arisen in the minds of both Mrs. Gardiner and the mother who went home under the impression the deceased was playing in the fields and would be home before long.

After waiting until about seven or eight in the evening, the subject of her non-appearance was discussed by the neighbours and fearing some foul play a party combined together and went in search. Soon after entering the hop garden previously mentioned, and on looking about, **the head of the missing child was picked up with a gash evidently inflicted by some sharp instrument from the mouth to the ear and another cut across the left temple it presented a hideous sight.** Other parts of the body with the exception of an arm and a foot, which were scattered about the garden, were found on Saturday evening. The parts of the body excepted were discovered early on Sunday morning. The mother on learning what had occurred became nearly frantic and rushed to communicate to her husband who was engaged at a cricket match, but before she got far she fell from excitement and had to be conveyed home. Messengers were immediately despatched to the father who on returning home seized a loaded gun and hastened to the hopgarden with the intention of shooting Baker but did not seem him and returned home presently.

CORONER'S INQUEST

Alton, Tuesday evening. This morning Mr. Robert Harfield, the deputy coroner for the county opened an inquiry at the Duke's Head Inn into the cause of the death of Fanny Adams, aged eight years and four months, whose body was found dismembered in a hop garden near this town on the afternoon of Saturday last. The jury proceeded to view the remains of the child and the accused man was brought in handcuffed. After hearing evidence· as to the finding of the remains Maurice Biddle, a clerk to Messrs. Clement, solicitors, at Alton stated the accused was in the office about six o'clock and told witness about the women speaking to him of the child. He said it would be very awkward for him if the girl was murdered. They went over to the Swan for a glass of ale and Baker said he was going away on Monday. Baker said he would go

with him.

William Walker said he found a large stone in the hop garden (stone produced). There was long hair on it and it was close to the spot where the head was found.

Mr. Superintendent Cheyney said that having heard of the murder he went to Baker's office, that person having been last seen with the children, and on telling him of the charge he said "I know nothing about it."

Evidence was given of the finding of two eyes. They were found in the Wey near the place of the murder. The Coroner then asked the accused if he decided to say anything to which Baker replied "No Sir, only that I am innocent." The Coroner then summed up with great care and returned a verdict of "Wilful murder against Frederick Baker for killing and slaying Fanny Adams."

The warrant was then made out for the committal of the miscreant to Winchester Gaol.

NEWGATE—TUESDAY MORNING

The last act of the Whitechapel tragedy has been played out. The closing scenes took place within the strong walls of Newgate; the hero (for many have endeavoured to make him the hero of an hour) suffered the extreme penalty of the law for a cruel and cowardly murder. In the grey hours of the early dawn death hovered around the couch of Henry Wainwright. The guilty man awoke on the morning of the 21st, to meet death face to face. Our artist had endeavoured to realise the situation by the aid of his graphic pencil. The execution of the unhappy wretch is thus described by a contemporary:

"The freshness of the morning seems to have been scared away from the place by that dismal shed standing in one corner, or rather by what that shed contains. A heavy beam some nine or ten feet from the ground is supported on stout up-rights, and from its centre drop half a dozen iron links with a coiled rope attached. That is all, and yet a more saddening sight cannot be found within the vast circle of London boundaries. Dismally tolls the bell; ten minutes more, five minutes, one minute—the clock strikes eight. Scarcely has the last sound died away when a heavy door creaks, there is a noise of feet, a voice proclaims the glad tidings of the Resurrection, and the prison chaplain enters the shed, followed by the hangman and Wainwright walking side by side. All eyes on the doomed man; all ears stretched to hear the slightest sound that may fall from his lips. Not a sound comes. Pinioned tightly as he is, Wainwright advances with firm and even step, and stands underneath the fatal beam facing the spectators. **Not a muscle of his face quivers; not a sign does he show of the pent up emotions that must be raging within him. Once or twice something like a smile seems to flit across his face as he stands there, calm and impassive, resolutely crushing down every exhibition of feeling that might be considered to suggest either guilt or innocence. Not for** **long is his face to be seen. Marwood soon covers it with the cap of doom; the rope is adjusted; the chaplain and executioner step back; and within a moment Henry Wainwright swiftly drops from view below the platform of the scaffold.** The rope quivers for a minute or two, when the spectators again begin whispering to one another, and the spell of seeing a man put to death is broken. After hanging the usual time the body was cut down in the presence of the prison officers.

All the arrangements were admirably carried out and the courtesy of the prison authorities to such as had cards of admission deserved every praise.

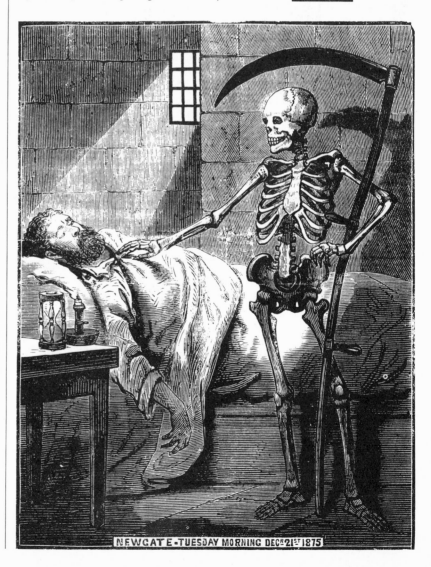

NEWGATE—TUESDAY MORNING DEC^R 21ST 1875

EXECUTION OF WIGGINS
Fearful Struggle on the Scaffold

On Tuesday morning John Wiggins, a lighterman, who was convicted at the last sittings of the Central Criminal Court, of the murder of a young woman named Agnes Oates, with whom he had co-habited in Limehouse, in July last, underwent the punishment of death in front of the gaol of Newgate.

There were probably never fewer people assembled at an execution in London. By seven o'clock and sometime afterwards, the whole length of the Old Bailey from Ludgate Hill nearly as far as the governor's house, was less crowded than on an ordinary day, and there was no difficulty in reaching the scaffold. This was attributed partly to the then approach-

ing execution of Bordier at Horsemonger-lane gaol, which had the effect, though it would not take place until two hours afterwards, of dividing the crowd. Nor was an assemblage of people collected at an execution ever more orderly perhaps.

The sheriffs (Alderman Stone and Mr. McArthur), with the undersheriffs, arrived at the prison shortly before eight o'clock. Forming themselves into a procession, with the governor of Newgate, the prison surgeon, the chaplain, and the representatives of the press, they walked to an open yard at the back of the governor's residence. There they halted a few moments, and then the convict attended by two warders,

passed before them to the pressroom, followed by the authorities. He was cool and collected and easily submitted himself to the process of pinioning, but complained once or twice that he was being too tightly bound. This process over the Rev. Mr. Lloyd Jones, the ordinary, addressed a few words of consolation to him, after which the convict said he wished to address the crowd outside. The governor told him he would not have an opportunity of doing that, and that what he had to say he had better say at once in the presence of the representatives of the press. The convict then said "I am entirely innocent of the charge for which I am about to die. I can assure you on my dying oath I never did it. I can go with a clear conscience and a clear heart to my Almighty Maker. It was her that cut my throat and then cut her own. I never lifted a hand or a finger to her, with my dying breath."

With that the prison bell began to

toll, and the convict was escorted to the scaffold, which he ascended with a light step, attended by the ordinary and the executioner. There a very unusual and a very painful scene occurred. The crowd, on seeing the convict, became very excited, and he began to resist the efforts of Calcraft to place him below the beam. First one of the stalwart prison officers and then another were summoned to assist in restraining him, until four or five of them, with the executioner, were upon the scaffold at one time. **After the cap had been drawn over his face, the convict shouted to the crowd "I am innocent: on my dying oath, I am innocent. Cut my head off, but don't hang me. I am innocent." By the motion of his lips he managed to work the cap off part of his mouth and he continued addressing the crowd, to declare his innocence again and again. Though his arms were pinioned at the elbows, he managed to clutch hold of the rope by which he was about to be suspended, and to hold it for some moments with a firm grasp, swaying himself about, and resisting the attempts of the warders to place him upon the drop, shouting the while that he was innocent. At length he was overcome by sheer force; the rope was adjusted, the drop fell, and the convict soon ceased to live. To the last he declared he was innocent.**

Since his trial the convict has availed himself of every opportunity to asseverate his innocence in various terms, and that the woman attempted to cut his throat and then cut her own. But there is a strong feeling in the public mind, nevertheless, and especially among the prison authorities, that he committed the murder. On Saturday he was visited by his father, a man upwards of seventy, and during the interview the father repeatedly urged him "to die like man and Christian." The old man then knelt down, and, in his own simple, homely language, offered up a prayer for his son. The convict had previously seen his brother and his sister-in-law. He was constantly in communication with the ordinary after his conviction, and by the prison authorities was regarded as a man of irascible temper. On Monday the ordinary had an interview with him and sought to prepare him for death. At times while it lasted the convict was amenable to the exhortations of the rev. gentleman, and at others he rose from his seat and walked about his cell with an air of determination as if it should not contain him.

A BOY MISTAKEN FOR A CROW

AWFUL CRUELTY TO AN IDIOT BOY

At the Sheffield Town Hall, Bridget McMahon, of Westbar, Sheffield, was committed for trial on a charge of horrible cruelty to her idiot boy, aged four. A neighbour's evidence showed that on the night of May 6th, prisoner was drunk, and witness saw prisoner throw the child who was quite naked, on the fire, which was a large one. The child fortunately rebounded on the fender, but was terribly burned all over the body. It was taken to the workhouse infirmary.

KILLED BY A CRICKET BALL

On Saturday last, a cricketer named James Styant was struck in the eye by a ball delivered with terrific force by the bowler. The ill-fated batsman fell to the earth with a deep groan, and expired about two hours after the accident.

AWFUL CRUELTY TO AN IDIOT BOY-

A BOY MISTAKEN FOR A CROW

A most unfortunate mistake occurred a few days ago by which the life of a little boy is imperilled, and we hope the case will act as a warning to rash and inexperienced sportsmen. The facts are briefly as follows. A boy who had climbed up a tree at Hayling Island was accidentally shot by a gentleman who was out shooting and mistook the poor little fellow for a young crow. The boy was removed to Portsmouth Hospital where he lies in a dangerous condition.

Singular Fatality

A woman named Godel, residing in Hill Street, St. Heliers, whilst removing her household goods on Friday, for greater speed, pitched a mattress out of an upper storey window. It alighted on a little boy who was passing, knocked him down, and broke one of his thighs, besides inflicting other injuries.

FIVE CHILDREN THROWN INTO A WELL

The following facts are given regarding a tragedy at Foxdale, Isle of Man. A farmer and miner of that place named Killey, who had for some time been unsettled in his reason, deliberately threw five of his children into a well near his own house and then jumped in himself. He had previously threatened to kill his wife.

A neighbour, attracted by the cries, hurried to the spot and other aid having been procured the bodies were drawn from the well when, extraordinary to say, two of the children were still alive. Efforts were made to restore animation to the other bodies, but in vain, the unfortunate man and the other three children being dead. One of the children rescued has since been seized with tetanus, or lock-jaw, and little hopes are entertained for its recovery.

It is stated that Killey's insanity commenced about five weeks ago and arose from a severe fall he sustained while returning home in a state of intoxication. Within the last few days his wife had been greatly alarmed at his talk.

On Friday afternoon, while three of his children were playing in the garden, he went out to them and the wife was alarmed to hear them crying. He turned to his wife and said we are all to go together and snatching the infant from her threw it into the well. A man named Slimm got into the bucket and was lowered into the well. He found four of the children floating on the water and grasped the child nearest to him and was hoisted up. Again and again he descended each time bringing up a child until he had brought up four in all. In about an hour after this ladders were procured and the two remaining bodies brought up.

An inquest was held on Saturday by the High Bailiff of Douglas. The jury returned a verdict that the three children had been drowned by James Killey whilst he was in a state of temporary insanity, and that he had drowned himself while he was in the same state. They appended to their verdict an expression of sympathy with the bereaved widow and of the admiration of the gallant conduct of Slimm.

FIVE CHILDREN THROWN INTO A WELL

PLACING AN OLD WOMAN ON THE FIRE

At the Birmingham Police Court, on Friday, a young man, named James Flint, of Fox-street, apparently about twenty years of age, was charged with violently assaulting an old woman, named Rosina Bibb, a widow, also of Fox Street, with intent to do her grievous bodily harm.

Complainant stated the defendant had been "keeping company" with her daughter against her (complainant's) wishes. On Saturday night he entered her house and commenced to illuse her in a shocking manner. He first knocked her down then commenced to kick her, and after this he tried to roast her upon the fire. He put her upon the fire once, but she succeeded in getting off, after being badly burned. He then caught hold of

her again, and tried three more times to put her upon the fire and he would have kept her upon the fire if she had not called for help. She was bruised all over her body from the kicks she received, and burnt, besides receiving a black eye from a kick while she was upon the floor.

In reply to the charge, defendant said the complainant was drunk, and struck him upon the nose with a poker.

Complainant denied this and said she could call a woman who had taken her off the fire.

Defendant: She was drunk and struck me with the poker, and also took the fender to me.

Mr. Kynnersley: Well even suppose she was drunk, and did strike you, you had no reason to abuse her in the disgraceful way you did. You must pay 40/- and costs or go to gaol for one month. Defendant: I have got no money—Mr. Kynnersley: Then go to gaol. Prisoner was then removed.

MURDER
AT
WEST
BROMWICH
Shocking barbarity

About half past five on Sunday morning, a supposed murder, attended with terrible cruelty, was discovered at the Hall End Pits, belonging to Mr. Alford, at Church Lane, West Bromwich. About the time named Isaac Blocksidge, an engine tenter, employed at the pits, having attended to his engine, went to the hovel on the bank in order to call up a man named Joseph Marshall, about fifty years of age, who was better known as "lame Joe" who has been employed at that pit and several others in the neighbourhood for many years as a labourer. As soon as he looked into the hovel, a most horrible sight presented itself. **The old man was on the ground at the front of a large fire, from which he was separated only by a few feet, and his right side was covered with**

fire, which had apparently been taken from the fireplace for the purpose and his flesh was literally being roasted. He removed the body from the fire and immediately ran for some water in order to extinguish the flames. It need hardly be stated, after having said that the body had suffered such inhuman treatment, that life was extinct.

On examining the poor fellow it was found that he was terribly burnt all over the right side and various other parts of the body. His stockings had been burned off his legs, and his leather belt so far consumed that only two pieces remained. Deceased had also several holes in his head which, it is supposed, were inflicted by a hammer or two rakes which were found in the hovel. The face of deceased presented an appearance of intense suffering. He left eye was closed, his right one open; and one of his hands was very much contracted. Parts of the body were entirely

consumed. The general supposition is that deceased was killed and that the murderer afterwards determined to consume the body. Information was at once given to the police, and Superintendent Woollaston and Police Constable McHarg visited the place, which was soon an object of intense interest in the neighbourhood. A labourer named John Higgison, aged fifty years, has been taken into custody on suspicion of being concerned in the deed, but in the present state of the case the police decline to furnish the press with any information as to the nature of the evidence to be produced against the prisoner who on being taken into custody said he knew nothing about the horrible business. We are informed that deceased was seen outside the hovel at half past two in the morning, and there is some talk in the neighbourhood of him and the prisoner having had a quarrel some short time ago, but of the truth of this we know nothing. We also hear that he and the

deceased were seen drinking together at a public house on Saturday evening.

On Tuesday afternoon, at about three o'clock, an inquest was opened on the body of Mr. Hooper, Coroner at the Nag's Head, Church Lane, West Bromwich. There was a crowd round the house during the whole of the proceedings. The foreman of the jury was Mr. Parish and having been sworn, they proceeded to view the body, which was in an outhouse near the public house. The horrible state and appearance of deceased nearly overcame some of the jurymen. The jury, having returned, evidence was taken as to the identification of the body.

Isaac Blocksidge, engine tenter, said "I work at the Hall End Colliery, and knew Joseph Marshall deceased, very well. Deceased was generally employed as a collier and was about fifty years of age. I have known him about fifteen years and he mostly lived in the hovel at the colliery. It is

SHOCKING BARBARITY AT WEST BROMWICH

the dead body of Marshall which the jury have just seen. I last saw him alive on Saturday night about eight o'clock, in this public house. He was then in very good health, and as far as I could see, sober.''

The Coroner said it was not his intention to take any evidence that day beyond identifying the body, as he thought the ends of justice would be better met, for various reasons, which he did not feel disposed to state at that moment, by having an adjournment of the inquest. He would first ask the jury if they decide to ask the witness any questions, merely reminding them at the same time that he would be brought before them again. He did not know whether the jurymen would like to see the hovel where Marshall was found, but if so the police would accompany them there when they had decided upon the adjournment. The Coroner then decided to adjourn the enquiry until Friday next at three o'clock.

The witness was bound over to appear in the sum of £20 and each of the jurymen in the sum of £10 and the proceedings terminated.

DESTRUCTIVE FIRE IN THE STRAND

On Monday morning, shortly after two o'clock, a destructive fire broke out in the "Red Lion" tavern in the Strand, which was entirely destroyed before an engine could be got to play on it. The first intimation of the fire seems to have been given by the volumes of smoke pouring out of the house. This drew the attention of a police-man on duty who immediately sprang his rattle, and, aided by one or two comrades, did all he could to arouse the inmates. The nearest fire escape was sent for and the engines from Chandos Street. In a few minutes piercing screams from the women were heard to proceed from the upper part of the house, and before the position of these poor creatures could be discerned through the smoke, one of the barmaids named Pritchard, finding that to remain where she was any longer was certain death, threw herself from an upper window to the pavement below. She fell with a dull, heavy thud and remained insensible until removed to Charing Cross Hospital.

Fortunately three other barmaids and inmates found their way to the roof and got thence to that of the next house. There they implored help which could not be rendered to them and they were only kept from precipitating themselves into the street by the persuasions of the people who assembled who assured the frantic creatures that the escapes were coming. After what seemed to be a serious delay an escape did come, and the man in charge after finding that one fly ladder was too short, threw up another which reached the parapet. He then mounted and bore one of the females down on his shoulders. A second got on the ladder herself and was assisted down in safety. Another escape then came and the man in charge mounted more quickly than his fellow and assisted down the third female. After the last person was rescued a steam fire engine came from Chandos Street, and last of all came the turncock. With extraordinary rapidity the flames were subdued, but not till the house was entirely burnt through. A large quantity of spirits on the premises aided the fire in its fierceness and much alarmed the spectators by the constant explosions of the barrels as the fire reached them. The office of the ECONOMIST newspaper was much injured. The women who were rescued were sheltered in the house of Mr. Jacobs, a hosier, opposite. It was stated that the landlord and landlady were absent at Gravesend on a holiday.

A CASK OF WHISKEY ON FIRE

On Friday, last week, Dr. Hardwicke opened an inquest at the Coroner's Court, Clerkenwell, on the body of Mr. Christopher Shoesmith, aged sixty, the proprietor of the "Royal Midshipman" Tavern, Clerkenwell. The deceased was engaged in knocking a tap into a large barrel of whiskey, when the tap split in two and the spirit began to run out. The barrel was turned on end, when the bung flew out and the whiskey flew all over the cellar. It was dark and the potman and deceased most unwisely called for a light, when, a candle being brought, the vapour of the whiskey ignited and the whole place was ablaze. Deceased and the potman made their escape by the trap door, but the former was so horribly burned that he died shortly afterwards. Verdict accidental death.

A CASK OF WHISKEY ON FIRE – DREADFUL DEATH

FEARFUL WIFE BEATING

On Thursday at the Thames Police Court, W. Barrett, labourer, was charged with assaulting his wife in a very brutal manner.

Mr. Smith, surgeon, said three of the woman's ribs were fractured, and that she was covered with weals and contusions. She could not leave the London hospital at present and must remain there under medical treatment for sometime longer.

McKay, a detective officer, said that a few nights ago prisoner came home with a large horsewhip and flogged his wife who was in bed, and had no other garment on but her chemise. The poor creature, who is seven months advanced in pregnancy, could offer no resistance. He flogged her "within an inch of her life", he trampled upon her and broke three of her ribs, and she was removed to the London Hospital bruised and shattered all over her body.

Prisoner on the first examination muttered that his wife was in the habit of getting drunk.

Mr. Bensom remanded him for a week.

MIRACULOUS ESCAPE FROM A FIRE

On Monday night last an extraordinary and exciting scene was witnessed at Lurgo. A fire broke out in the premises of Mrs. McPherson between nine and ten o'clock. The flames spread with such astonishing rapidity that in less than half an hour the basement storey and the one immediately above it were completely gutted. Happily the occupants of the house succeeded in making their escape, with the exception of a work girl named Jane Wilson, who was in a front room in the upper part of the premises. The poor girl ran towards the windows which she opened, at the same time screaming loudly for assistance. Those below implored her not to make any attempt to jump into the street. Ladders were procured but none proved long enough to reach the room occupied by Jane Wilson. Eventually a young man named Thomas Metcalf, a carpenter by trade, volunteered his assistance. **He spliced two ladders together, and at the imminent risk of his own life, ascended, and succeeded in reaching the window, through which the flames were issuing. He contrived to clutch hold of the girl Wilson, and brought her safely into the street below, amidst the cheers of hundreds of excited spectators.**

FEARFUL WIFE BEATING

woman was found sitting in a chair and bleeding profusely from wounds in the head. Her hair was matted with blood and it was impossible to see the extent of her injuries. Shortly after admission to the infirmary Mrs. Deacon was seen by the house surgeon and she died about an hour and a half after being received at that Institution. Much sympathy is felt for the step-daughter who is spoken of as an industrious girl and the poor young creature expressed her belief that Deacon was not drunk when he committed the savage crime. The murder has created intense excitement in the neighbourhood, which is densely populated.

FATAL QUARREL

A few days ago at Teroma, a sad termination to a quarrel took place. It appears that a husband and wife (we suppress their names for special reasons) were walking on the heights during which time a violent altercation took place. The husband was seen to strike his wife twice. In a few minutes after this the ill-fated man fell over the rocks into the turbid stream below. It is reported that he was pushed over by his enraged partner; but we hope that this supposition will turn out to be an erroneous one.

FRIGHTFUL WIFE MURDER IN BRISTOL

Bristol has again become the scene of a cold-blooded and deliberate murder tragedy bearing striking resemblance to the last two cases of homicide which occurred in that city.

It appears that a young man named Edward Deacon, twenty-seven years old and a shoemaker by trade, lived with his wife and a daughter by a previous marriage, a young woman named Ann Hallett, in a small cottage in Barton Street. The husband was a drunkard while the wife was an industrious and well conducted woman, working with her daughter by the aid of a sewing machine, as a tailoress. Deacon for some reason unexplained was absent from his wife for five years and they resumed co-habitation last Christmas. Since that period however, Deacon appears to have worked but seldom and he and his wife frequently quarrelled. On Wednesday afternoon they were the sole occupants of the house, the daughter having gone out and about

half-past four Deacon borrowed a hatchet from a woman to chop some wood. Five minutes later neighbours were alarmed by cries for help from Mrs. Deacon and the unfortunate

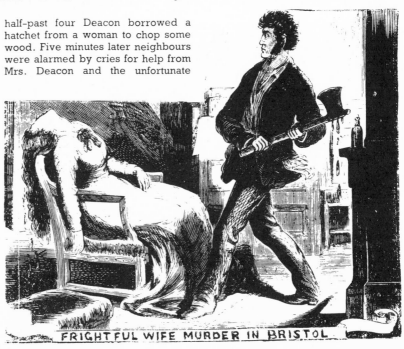
FRIGHTFUL WIFE MURDER IN BRISTOL

HAIRDRESSING EXTRAORDINARY

On Friday, a hairdresser named Lew Eccles, was fined 20/- and costs by the Huddersfield borough magistrates for cutting off the hair of a girl aged nine years, who had gone to his shop to have her hair dressed.

FEARFUL TRAGEDY
OF A LUNATIC STEPMOTHER

On Monday morning a sad occurrence took place at the village of Stow Bedon, on the road leading from Attenborough to Caston—the murder of a child by its mother, and an attempt on the life of a second child, the fate of which is still uncertain. It appears that Mary Hanner, the mother in question, is the wife of a labourer, and was predisposed to fits of insanity, having, in fact been confined for some time in a lunatic asylum, and even very lately attempted suicide. On Sunday night she complained of feeling ill, but the next morning, when her husband was leaving for work, she said she felt better. In the house with her were three children one an idiot, eighteen years of age, a daughter of Mr. Hanner by his first wife; another little girl of five years old; and the third an infant aged fifteen months.

Rising from her bed, the wretched woman seems to have gone from the room and entered the room where the idiot girl was sleeping, and tying her arms behind her with great care, pulled her on to the floor and cut her throat from ear to ear. The gash thus made was fearful, and although it was sewn up very shortly afterwards and every effort is being made to save the life of the poor creature, it is feared all efforts will be in vain. From the room where this act was committed, the mother went to the place where the infant was sleeping, and cutting its throat killed it instantly.

While doing so the little girl of five years awoke, upon which the woman seized the child, and would have served it the same as the other but for her plaintive appeals to be allowed to live as her "pet". The mother's feelings appear somewhat to have returned, and she desisted from her diabolical attempts, so she threw down the knife, and taking the child in her arms, carried it through the room where the idiot girl was lying wounded and out of doors to a neighbour's house, where she disclosed what had happened. It was quite the impression of the murderess that both her victims were dead; but as has been before stated, the eldest still lives, though in a most precarious condition. The woman is now in custody and will be brought before the magistrates at once.

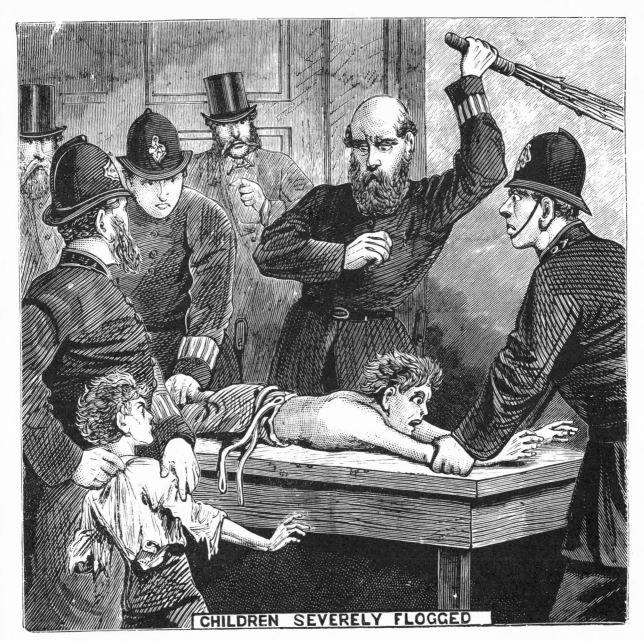

CHILDREN SEVERELY FLOGGED

Children severely *flogged*

Two ragged and helpless urchins, named John Levitt and Frank Rafferty, aged eleven and nine years respectively, were brought up in custody charged with stealing two pigeons, the property of Mr. John Rhodes of Knottingley, on the previous Thursday. It appears from the evidence of the prosecutor, that on the day in

question he had two pigeons that were valued at 3/6d. taken out during the day. On being apprehended by the police who found one of the pigeons at the house of Levitt's parents, the juvenile prisoners first denied stealing them, but afterwards confessed their guilt. Mrs. Levitt said she was the wife of a labourer and had four children. She had recently been very ill and during her sickness the boy had not behaved very well. Rafferty's mother informed the bench that she was a hawker, and had eight children all of whom attended the Church Sunday School.

In addressing the parents of the boys Mr. Peel said "It's a serious thing to bring up children in the way that you are doing and you don't

know what it might lead to. We must punish them and we must send them to a reformatory, but we now order them to receive ten strokes each with the birch rod." The punishment was not, however, inflicted with a birch rod as ordered, but with a number of strong willows plaited, about four feet in length, which were fastened together at the extreme end with a piece of hemp cord. The backs of the destitute, miserable and helpless urchins were bared from the shoulders to the calves of the legs. They were than stretched upon a wooden table with a police officer at one end holding down the head and arms, whilst another member of the force officiated at the other end by holding down the legs and feet.

Whilst held in this position Police-Sergeant Grimshaw wielded the heavy weapon across each of the prostrate forms, taking Rafferty, who was the younger of the two, first. The ten blows dealt in his case were excessively severe and the piteous cries of the helpless child during the first two or three strokes were heart-rending to hear. After these, however, he was unable to scream, and at the conclusion he was unequal to the task of readjusting his rags, and reeled against the back of a seat in a fainting condition. Levitt was next stripped and placed upon the table in the manner described, but for some reason unknown the blows in this case were dealt with less severity, and the miserable youngster was enabled to scream with increasing piteousness, until sometime after the tenth lash was inflicted. This is the second case of child flogging ordered by the West Riding Justices during the past two months.

Flogging Garrotters at Leeds

On Saturday afternoon eight men who at the recent Leeds gaol delivery had been convicted of robberies with violence were punished with 24 strokes each of the cat o' nine tails in the Borough Gaol, as ordered by Mr. Justice Lush. About eighteen inches in length, each lash has at the end three strings of whipcord, with nine knots on each string, and it "told" with marked effect upon the bare shoulder of each criminal.

The following were the convicts who had to undergo punishment—Thomas Kilmartin aged 23, Hugh Gallagher of Leeds, Richard Walker aged 24 and Edward Till of Sheffield, James O'Brien and Thomas Cooper of Sheffield.

William Craven and James Holmes were in trouble for being concerned in garrotting and robbing John Gibson at Whitkirk.

Some of the convicts sobbed violently as if in extreme pain and writhed under the agony of more than eighteen strokes of the "cat".

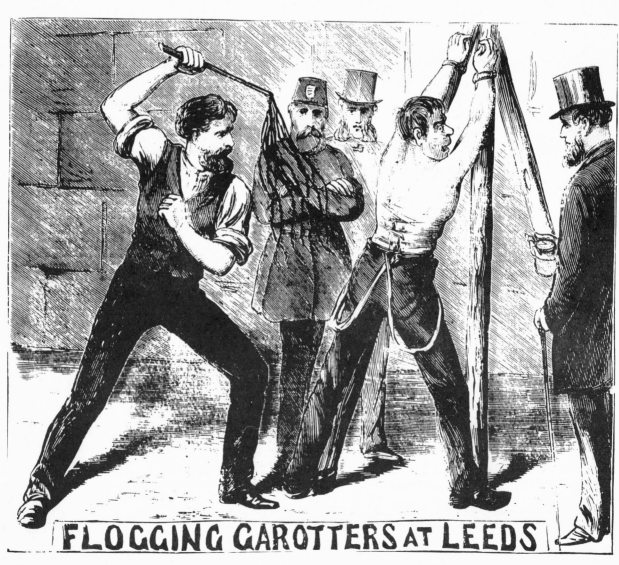

FLOGGING GAROTTERS AT LEEDS

A WIFE DRIVEN INSANE BY HUSBAND TICKLING HER FEET

On Thursday, last week, a very serious charge was preferred against a man named Michael Puckridge, who resides at Winbursh, a small village in Northumberland. The circumstances, as detailed before the board of guardians, are of a harrowing nature. It appears that Puckridge who has lived very unhappily with his wife, whose life he has threatened on more than one occasion. Most probably he had long contemplated the wicked design which he carried out but too successfully about a fortnight since. Mrs. Puckridge, who is an interesting looking young woman, has for a long time past suffered from varicose veins in the legs, her husband told her that he possessed an infallible remedy for this ailment. **She was induced by her tormentor to**

TICKLEING A WOMAN'S FEET - A WIFE DRIVEN MAD

SINGULAR METHOD OF EXECUTION

allow herself to be tied to a plank, which he placed across two chairs. When the poor woman was bound and helpless, Puckridge deliberately and persistently tickled the soles of her feet with a feather. For a long time he continued to operate upon his unhappy victim, who was rendered frantic by the process. Eventually she swooned, whereupon her husband released her. It soon became too manifest that the light of reason had fled. Mrs. Puckridge was taken to the workhouse where she was placed with other insane patients. A little girl, a niece of the woman, spoke to one or two of the neighbours saying her aunt had been tied to a plank and her uncle cruelly illtreated her.

An inquiry was instituted and there is every reason to believe that Mrs. Puckridge had been driven out of her mind in the way described but the result of the investigation is not yet known.

A strange and dreadful mode of executing criminals exists in Persia. The Shah is supposed to witness these executions. "During my stay in Teheran" says Mr. Fowler, in his interesting work, "a culprit was suspended by the legs from two poles, and literally cut in half by the henchman in the royal presence.

"This mode of punishment is common in Persia, and it is called the 'shekeh', and is performed by the chief executioner, a most important officer, and always His Majesty's person.

"They sometimes adopt the ancient method of execution, said to have been first tried upon Bessus, the murderer of Darius—that of having two young trees brought together by main strength at their summits, and then fastened with cords. The culprit being brought out and his legs tied with ropes at the top of the trees, the cords which fasten them together are then cut, and by the power and elasticity of their spring the body of the culprit is immediately torn asunder, and the different parts are left attached to each tree separately."

JAPANESE PUNISHMENT FOR ADULTERY

JAPANESE PUNISHMENT FOR ADULTERY

Mr. Hapgood, an English traveller who is just returned from Japan, has forwarded us some very interesting notes which he made during his travels. One refers to a custom which forms the subject of our illustration.

The facts are as follows:—

A man and a woman were charged with adultery. The guilt of both parties was proved to the satisfaction of the judges. The punishment awarded to the offend-ers is perfectly horrible. The woman was condemned to be torn to pieces by wild bullocks; the sentence passed on the man was crucifixion. The barbarous punish-ments were inflicted on both offenders. The man was crucified and while writhing in agony, his partner in guilt was torn to pieces before his eyes, by oxes. Such monstrous inhumanity appears almost incredible.

LYNCHING FOUR MEN

A despatch to the San Francisco Bulletin, gives an account of the lynching of four men in Tucson, Arizona:

"At mid-night on Wednesday, Vicente Hernandez, a pawnbroker and his wife, were murdered by having their skulls crushed in with a club and a jugular vein cut with a knife. 900 dollars reward were subscribed by citizens for the capture of the criminals responsible and six men were arrested on suspicion. The principal murderer, a Mexican, named Leonardo Cordova, confessed, fully exposing his associates, one of whom subsequently confessed. The three were compelled to expose the hiding place of the plunder. Next morning a determination was expres-

LYNCHING FOUR MEN

sed to hang the three murderers of Hernandez and his wife, and also to hang John Willis, who killed Robert Swope at Sanford, in November 1872, and indicted there for in March 1873. The arrangements were completed next morning. Two posts, forked at the top, were planted in the ground near the gaol door, and upon them was placed a pole about twelve feet in length. To this pole four ropes were fastened, with nooses to each, and two waggons were drawn beneath. The Catholic priest desiring to give consolation to the doomed men, was given the time desired. The four doomed men, John Willis, Leonardo Cordova, Clementie Lopez, and Jesus Saquaripa, were brought out of gaol with bandages over their eyes, put in the waggons, the ropes adjusted to their necks, waggons drawn out, and all four hung side by side.''

SUICIDE FROM WATERLOO BRIDGE

This melancholy case has been fully commented upon by the Press and the following report appeared in our issue of last week:

"On Monday evening an inquest was held at Essex Street, Strand, to inquire into the circumstances of the death of the young woman who threw herself off Waterloo Bridge on the afternoon of the preceding Thursday, and who was presumed, from a letter which was found in her possession, to be an American governess named Alice Blanche Oswald. Elizabeth Caith, a Coffee House keeper of Shadwell said she had seen the body of the deceased who was a lodger of hers and went by the name of Lockie. She did not give me any Christian name. A gentleman called and went out with her once, and the day before a lady called and went out with her. She said she was a governess and a lady had engaged her for twelve months, but when she got to the place it was so hard she could not stop. She said she went to London to try to get the American Consul to pay her passage back. She came to me as Miss Lockie and seemed to be about twenty-five. Last Thursday she had a letter addressed to Mrs. Oswald and this I gave to her. She had apparently been expecting someone and when the letter came she was much upset. She commented "I ought to have had this letter an hour ago". She seemed in good health and spirits and she went out. She did not seem to be in want but said she would like a situation in England rather than returning to America.

William King, inspector of the Thames Police, searched the body of the deceased and the following letter was produced:

"The crime I am about to commit and for which I must suffer hereafter is nothing to compare to my present misery. Alone in London, not a penny, or a friend to advise or lend a helping hand, tired and weary with looking for something to do, failing in every way, foot-sore and heart weary, I prefer death to the dawning of another wretched morning. I have

only been in Britain nine weeks. I came as a Nursery Governess with a lady from America to Wick, in Scotland, whence she discharged me refusing to pay my passage back, giving me my wages which amounted to £3 10s. After my expenses in London I found myself in this great city with only 5/-. Now I am destitute. Oh God of heaven have mercy upon a poor helpless sinner. I cannot tread the path of sin for my dead mother will be watching me. Fatherless, motherless, home I have none. May all who hear of my end forgive me and may God almighty do so before whose bar I must so soon appear. Farewell to all to this beautiful yet wretched world. ALICE BLANCHE OSWALD. P.S. I am twenty years old on the 14th of this month."

A verdict was returned "That the deceased committed suicide while in a state of temporary insanity."

THE BURNING OF A SHIP AND FIVE HUNDRED COOLIES

The Overland China Mail of May 12th, gives the testimony of the survivors of the coolie ship Don Juan, whose loss at sea with 650 coolies on board has already been reported. Leung Ashew, a native of Sunniug, twenty years old, describes how he had been kidnapped at Macao, forced to sign a contract, and then sent, with others guarded by armed men, on board the vessel. He then said:

"On the third day after we sailed, shortly after our breakfast, there was a fire on board. The fire occurred in the aft part, in a room adjoining our hold. The smoke came into our hold in a great volume; it had a strong smell of gunpowder. I heard no explosion whatever before the alarm of fire. The hatch grating was never opened all the while. The smoke came in very thick and a great many were suffocated. More than one hour after the smoke first came into our hold the hatch grating was torn off, by one of the cooks, I believe. We all made a rush for the hatchway. When I came up the whole of the ship from

THE BURNING OF A SHIP AND FIVE HUNDRED COOLIES

the mainmast to the stern was one mass of flames. The foremast had not caught fire then. About twenty men clung to the rigging and others were holding to the bowsprit. I was holding on to the anchor chain. When the fire reached the woodwork which held the anchor chain. I tumbled into the sea with the anchor. I could swim a little and I swam to a burnt spar. I was carried so far from the burning ship that I could hardly see her. I was picked up by a fishing junk that passed in the evening of the same day the fire occurred. The junkmen wanted us to give them money before they would pick us up. I paid them five dollars and they picked me up, but refused to take in my companions, four in number, because they had no money to pay them. My treatment on board the fishing junk was very good but I could not eat as I was in great pain from my burns.''

The fire was apparently lighted with the purpose of forcing all those living overhead to go forward, and thus simplify the capture of the vessel. It is said that on being asked through the grating what they wanted, the coolies declared their intention of taking the ship. However, improbable this may appear, it is alleged the coolies openly stated their purpose. It is presumed that they expected the fire would be easily extinguished, and that they never anticipated the horrible death in store for them.

AN ENCOUNTER WITH A SEA DEVIL

We have received from the mate of an English trading vessel a rough sketch of "a monster of the deep", known by the title of a "Sea Devil" attacking a fishing smack. We are informed by our correspondent that he can vouch for the truth of the strange encounter, which is briefly described in the paper he forwarded with his sketch, and from which our engraving is taken. The apparently exaggerated description of the Sea Devil in The Toilers of the Sea loses much of its impossibility in one's mind after an inspection of a huge cephaloped now being shown in the house near the temple at Asaksa, Yedo. It seems that a fishing boat was seized by its tentacles whilst off the village of Kononoto, in the district of Kisaradzou, and that the boatmen killed the creature by repeated blows. Its length from the tail to the insertion of the tentacles is about sixteen feet, one of the arms is from the junction of the body to the sucker at its point nearly five feet. It must be borne in mind that the polypus has shrunk since its death, so that living it would probably measure considerably more. After this, even Bishop Eric Pontoppidau's kraken stories are almost credible.

JAPAN GAZETTE, April 23.

AN ENCOUNTER WITH A SEA DEVIL

HORRIBLE DISCOVERY
OF A GIRL EATEN BY RATS

A most appalling discovery was made last week in the town of Haverball. The circumstances of the case are both remarkable and horrible to the last degree. The facts are as follows: For some months past a man named William Laslett, his wife, and a daughter (a girl about thirteen years of age) have occupied two rooms on the basement storey of a house in Princes Street. Laslett, it appears, is a travelling hawker in the hardware line; he keeps a horse and cart, with which he travels from town to town, and has been accustomed to be absent from home six or eight weeks at a time. Occasionally he would take with him his daughter on his travelling expeditions, but more frequently his wife accompanied him. He left Princes-street with the latter seven

weeks ago, Jane Laslett the daughter, remaining behind. The young girl was seen by her neighbours for a few days after her parents had departed, when all of a sudden she was missed. The doors of both rooms in the occupation of the Lasletts were locked, and the natural inference was that Jane had left to join her parents, as she had been known to do so before on more than one occasion. Weeks passed over; the suspicions of the other occupants of the house that something was amiss became stronger every day. An unpleasant and sickening odour crept up the staircase and found its way into the the several apartments. On Monday last, a carpenter who occupied one of the upper rooms, was prevailed upon to break open the door which led to

those on the basement, whereupon he was horror-struck at the sight presented to him. Upon the door being burst open, a legion of rats scampered in all directions. The greater portion of the body of the poor girl had been devoured by the rats. The medical gentlemen who have since made a post-mortem examination, concur in the opinion that Jane Laslett died suddenly from disease of the heart of long standing—that her death had in all probability taken place some weeks back, since which time the rats had been feeding on the body. The father and mother have not yet returned, nor do the neighbours know where to communicate with them.

A BURGLAR

BITTEN BY A SKELETON

A "skeleton in the closet" is not generally considered a pleasant thing to have, but a recent occurrence in Greensburg, America, shows that it may sometimes answer a good purpose. We learn from the Philadelphia Medical Times that a burglar broke into a physician's office in the town and opening a closet (while his companion was in another part of the room) got his hands between the jaws of a skeleton, which being adjusted with a coil spring and kept open with a thread, closed suddenly on the intruding hand by the breaking of the thread. Startled at being thus seized he uttered a faint shriek, and when his companion turned the lantern towards him, and he beheld himself in the grim and grisly jaws of Death himself, he became so overpowered by fear that he fainted; and fell insensible to the floor, pulling the skeleton down upon him and making so much noise that his companion fled immediately. The doctor alarmed at the noise and confusion, hastened into the room and secured the terror stricken burglar, still held by the skeleton. Burglars who may have a design upon the tranquility or incumbrances of any of our households will take warning by the unhappy fate which befell one of "their comrades in arms" in a doctor's study at the other side of the Atlantic.

SHOCKING TREATMENT OF A LUNATIC

At the Notts Assizes on Saturday, before Baron Huddleston, George Goforth Wyer, a surgeon, practising at Eastwood, was charged with receiving into his house, which was not properly licensed, and taking charge of a lunatic named Selina Wyer (his sister) without having the requisite medical certificate, and he was further charged with abusing, ill-treating and neglecting the said lunatic. The prosecution was instituted by the Lunacy Commissioners. On the 29th February, Dr. Tate of the Nottingham Coppice Asylum, in accordance with an order which he had received from the Lord Chan-

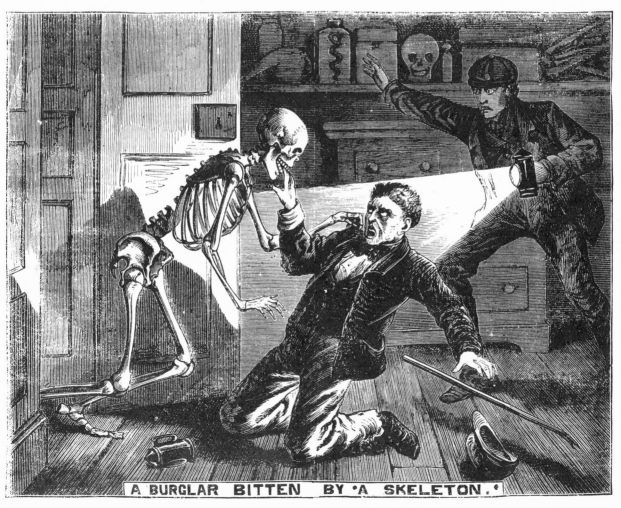

A BURGLAR BITTEN BY A SKELETON.

SHOCKING TREATMENT OF A LUNATIC BY A SURGEON

cellor, went to the house of the defendant who, it should be stated had received large sums of money from his father, a retired army surgeon, living at Whitchurch, Dorset, for taking care of his sister.

Dr. Tate, producing the order, asked to see the lunatic, and was taken by the defendant upstairs to an attic, the window of which was boarded up and in which there was no fire. All the furniture the room contained was a box and a trestle, and upon the latter a female was crouching, with her knees drawn up to her chin. She was quite naked with the exception of a small vest, which covered her shoulders and breast. She was in a very filthy state and an old woollen rug which was thrown over her was in a disgusting condition. She was very thin and feeble and was apparently unable to stand up. The defendant told her roughly to get up and she began to cry. Defendant pleaded guilty. It was urged in defence that he had suffered from sunstroke and was rather eccentric. He was sentenced to three months imprisonment.

GROSS INHUMANITY TO CHILDREN

ON Thursday afternoon a painful case of "chronic" starvation was heard at the Hyde Police Court. The case was one in which Thomas Whittaker, a bobbin maker, at Messrs. Hirst's Mill, Broadbottom, had been apprehended on a warrant which charged Whittaker that on

the 5th day of June, 1877, being the father, of Thomas, Charlotte, Ellen Ann and Louisa Whittaker, children of tender age under the care and control of the said Thomas Whittaker, unlawfully did neglect and refuse to find for the said children, sufficient meat, drink, wearing apparel, bedding and other necessities proper and requisite for the sustenance and support, clothing, covering and resting of the bodies of the said children, by means whereof they became sick, weak, ill, starved and

greatly emaciated in their bodies.

On opening the case with a review of the facts Captain Arrowsmith stated that the prisoner and the woman with whom he lived came originally from Oldham, but had been residing in Broadbottom for four years. He had lived with the woman as his wife, by whom he had three other children, which were well nourished, whereas the children whom he was charged with neglecting, his own children, and not those of the woman with whom he cohabited, were greatly emaciated, some of them had scarcely been seen by the neighbours for years and others of them had been seen to pick up potato peelings and wash and eat them.

At the end of the hearing the Chairman said the prisoner was responsible, and it was the most disgraceful case he had ever before him, and he did not believe there was such a thing at this day. After he had paid his rent he had almost £2. He would be sent to prison for six months with hard labour. Prisoner: Shall I be allowed to see my children before I go? He was answered in the affirmative, and in the cell, immediately after, he hugged and kissed each of them, cried, and so did the children.

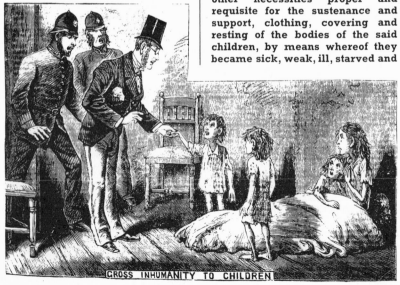

GROSS INHUMANITY TO CHILDREN

THE LAST MOMENTS OF

A GORILLA

Dr. Karl Nissle reports thus on the last moments of the gorilla at the Berlin Zoological Gardens. A few weeks after the deadly disease had made its appearance, the gorilla, hitherto full of power, petulence, elasticity and astuteness, the most splendid prototype of all quadromanes, became a most rueful figure to see. The sprightliness and life, and even the Director, was hardly noticed by his pet even after enticing it. Yet this bearing was by no means that of good temper, not even of resignation. The large clear eye of the gorilla reflected an almost frightful expression of deep disappointment—I would say contankerousness. Of the touching look of the dying chimpanzee, imploring as it were help from his attendant, there was no trace with Mafuka. The animal suffered because it could not help it—we may say with complete certainty that none could cure or alleviate its consumptive disease. This state continued unchanged until a few minutes before its death. When the Director once more stooped over his favourite Mafuka then put her arm round his neck, and for a while with her clear eyes had a deep glance at her faithful protector. Then she kissed him three times at short intervals, gently reclined on the couch, and once more shook hands with Schopf, by way of farewell, after many years happy life together, and quickly fell asleep to wake no more.

THE LAST MOMENTS OF A GORILLA

THRILLING ACCIDENT AT BOLTON

THRILLING ACCIDENT AT BOLTON

Perilous Fall of a Female Blondin

On Tuesday evening last week an exciting scene was witnessed at Bolton. In connection with Mr. Pablo Fanque's circus a female Blondin had been announced to give an outdoor performance. She was to walk along a rope stretched from the third storey of the Old Coronation Mills to the top of the circus, the height of the rope from the ground being about sixty feet and the distance to be gone over some eighty feet. About half past seven the woman set out from the window. She tripped along the rope for a few feet with a light and easy step. About fifteen feet from the starting point, however, she came to a thick knot, several inches long. She tried to cross it but failed and then turned back. A moment afterwards she resumed her journey. She approached the knot cautiously and partially crossed it; but just as her hindmost foot was leaving it she stumbled.

At once she threw aside her pole but by a desperate effort she grasped the rope. She is a strong muscular woman and she exerted herself greatly to regain her position on the rope; but despite her endeavours she remained suspended by the hands. The wildest excitement prevailed amongst the thousands of spectators. There were loud cries of "Lower the rope" and the rope was lowered by only a few feet. A number of men then massed themselves together directly below the woman and begged her to fall. She did as advised and was caught by the men, and although the distance she fell was almost fifty feet she sustained no injury beyond the fright and a shake.

A Ballet Girl Burnt to Death

An accident of a deplorable character occurred on Friday night at Day's Crystal Palace Concert Hall, Smallbrook Street. About a quarter to eleven, when the ballet scene, and when the whole of the ballet girls were on the stage, one of them named Fanny Smith, struck with a wand the wick of a lamp which was fixed on a pedestal about seven feet high. A portion of the wick, saturated with spirits of wine, fell upon her dress and it ignited directly, and in a moment she was enveloped in flames. She rushed on the stage and then off, and then on again, and was at length rolled in a man's coat, and the fire was extinguished, not until she was dreadfully, if not fatally burned all over the body. She was taken to the Queen's Hospital where she now lies in a very dangerous condition.

The sight of the girl in flames appeared to cause a panic amongst the audience who rushed wildly to the doors which, fortunately, had been opened to allow of the egress of the visitors. The entrance having been lately very much widened, the hall was soon cleared of the greater portion of the audience.

It is with feelings of deep regret that we record the death of the ill-fated ballet girl Fanny Smith, who died on Monday last, from the injuries sustained by burns at Day's Music Hall, Birmingham.

SUICIDE FROM THE BRIDGE AT CLIFTON, BRISTOL

A report of this melancholy affair appeared in our edition last week, which doubtless will be fresh in the memory of most of our readers. We subjoin, however, a resume of the facts:— A man was seen to get over the suspension bridge. The height of the structure is 245 feet above high water mark, and the low water point upon which the unhappy young man fell was some twenty feet below that. It would seem that the poor fellow paid his toll at the gate for crossing the bridge, and proceeded as far as the centre of the bridge on the upper or Bristol side, and that then, having denuded himself of his hat, coat and waistcoat, he clambered over the parapet and rushed to his death. He was seen by persons at the Hot-Wells to get over the rail of the bridge and hang on by both hands. In a few moments he released one of them and almost instantly was seen tumbling over and over through the air into the abyss below. Owing to some barricades which have been raised along the banks of the Avon to cover some extensive works going on in connection with the improvement and extension of the harbour, the persons on the Gloucestershire banks of the river did see him actually strike the mud, but Mr. Wilkinson the resident engineer of the port and pier railway, who happened to be passing, heard a loud "thud" or sound, which he at first supposed might have been caused by blasting the cliffs, and on running to an opening in the planks of the balustrade, he saw the poor fellow's body on the mud lying on his back. Mr. Wilkinson at once obtained the assistance of some of his men, and the body was got up and removed to "The General Draper Tavern" where it was handed in charge of the police.

THE SKELETON IN THE CUPBOARD

Our engraving represents a misadventure of so singular and alarming a nature that we are reminded thereby that "truth is stranger than fiction". This fact is forcibly impressed on all who take the trouble to note well the events which come under their personal observations. On Wednesday last week, a young woman named Emily Fitzpatrick, sustained a shock, through mere idle curiosity, that might well shake the nerves of the strongest of the opposite sex. Her uncle Mr. Murgatroyd, has but recently become the occupant and possessor of an old mansion situated at Perry Bar, Northamptonshire, which he purchased for a very inconsiderable sum. The house, prior to the purchase, was for many years

THE SKELETON IN THE CUPBOARD

A SPONGE DIVER SWALLOWED BY A SEA

ONSTER

tenanted by an eccentric gentleman who was a member of the medical profession. At one time it had the unenviable reputation of being haunted and the gossips in the neighbourhood one and all, declared that at midnight strange and unearthly sounds were heard to proceed from the doctor's house as it was termed by most of the neighbours. Despite these scandalous reports the doctor continued to live on, heedless of what he justly deemed absurd rumours, and died a few months ago at the ripe age of eighty-three. Soon after his decease the present owner took possession of the habitation, taking with him besides his wife and family, a favourite niece, whose adventure would have been an admirable subject for the magic pencil of Hans Holbein, whose "Dance of Death" was popular for so many years in this and other countries.

It appears notwithstanding its unenviable notoriety, both Mr. and Mrs. Murgatroyd contrived to make themselves very comfortable in their new habitation, despite its dark passages and gloomy appearance outside, and the labyrinth passages, quaint old cupboards and odd shaped wainscotted rooms contained within its walls. In one of the last named Miss Fitzpatrick discovered a small keyhole in one of the panels. She mentioned the circumstances to her aunt and uncle, saying that she believed there was a secret cupboard or passage in the room.

Mr. Murgatroyd ridiculed the idea, so his niece did not press the matter further. Her curiosity, however, was aroused and when Mr. and Mrs. Murgatroyd were out she took an opportunity on Wednesday week last of creeping upstairs with a lighted candle in one hand and all the keys she could collect in the other. For a long time she was engaged in trying to get one to fit, until at length success crowned her efforts, but the bolt of the lock would not turn—probably the inside was corroded with rust—but Miss Fitzpatrick persevered until the difficulty was overcome. After this feat had been accomplished the door would not readily open. The young lady, however, was not to be baffled—she tugged at the door with all her strength until it eventually burst suddenly open. **A grim and ghastly skeleton fell forward and seemed to her bewildered imagination to grasp her in a deadly embrace. Her situation at this time was of a nature so appalling that it is no matter for surprise that she screamed loud enough to alarm the whole neighbourhood.**

Hewson, an old and faithful servant of the family, rushed to Miss Emily's assistance. Upon her arrival she found the latter in a state of unconsciousness, her young mistress having swooned in consequence of the great fright to which she had been subjected. The skeleton was stretched at full length on the floor of the apartment.

Miss Emily Fitzpatrick is still weak; indeed she is almost in a prostrate condition; but her medical attendant gives hope that, with due care and attention, she will ultimately recover.

A SPONGE DIVER SWALLOWED BY A SEA MONSTER

A very terrible story reaches us from the Holy Land. There can be no doubt that in the depths of the sea there exist uncouth fantastic monsters, which like the Great Sea Serpent and Devil Fish, are only seen occasionally by mariners. It is difficult to persuade some persons that there is any truth in the story of the Sea Serpent. Nevertheless it seems most improbable that so many witnesses can be found to vouch for the truth of the statement. The monster depicted was seen by some score of persons or more. Mr. T. S. Jago, Her Majesty's Vice Consul at Beirout,

in his report of the trade of Syria in 1875, states that the crop of sponges were very deficient, in consequence of the appearance of a sea monster, alleged to be equal in size to a small boat, in the neighbourhood of Batroun, Mount Lebanon, the chief sponge fishing locality. The actual injury done appears to have been confined to one man, but as he was "swallowed whole", according to the testimony of his fellow workers, there was such a fright among the divers that many of them ceased operations, and the deficiency in the quantity of sponges obtained ran prices up.

TERRIBLE SUFFERING OF TWO SHIPWRECKED SAILORS

Information has just been received of the loss at sea of the British barque "County of Richmond", while on a voyage from New York to St. Thomas, with a cargo of coal. She had a crew of nine men and was commanded by Captain R. McDonald. All were lost with the exception of the first mate, Samuel McDonald (a brother of the Captain) and a seaman named Harry Lang. The vessel it appeared left New York on the 3rd October, and soon afterwards she encountered a series of heavy gales with very high seas. On the 14th, she was found to be so badly strained as to be in immediate danger of foundering. The crew, therefore, prepared to leave her.

One of the two boats had been smashed by the sea and an attempt was made to lower the second one, but this was almost instantly swamped. Very soon after this, the barque went down, stern foremost, drawing the unfortunate crew down
with her. The first officer, just before the vessel foundered, got hold of a ladder, to which he lashed two planks. This he threw overboard and sprang after it. He was tossed twenty feet from it by an immense wave but managed to get hold of it and as he did so he saw another man, Lang, also holding on. They both kept hold of the ladder until the forecastle deck which had floated from the wreck, drifted near to them, when they let go and swam to it. The deck formed a raft about thirteen feet long and eight broad, and was a comparatively safe refuge, though it was tossed about in the heavy sea and the two men had to lash themselves to it to prevent being washed off.

When they gained the raft they looked around for the rest of the crew but only a few spars were in sight, and it was evident that McDonald and Lang were the only survivors from the wreck.

McDonald had been suffering for sometime before from a sore leg, and the salt water increased the pain very much. To relieve this, and to protect his leg, he took off his flannel undershirt and wrapped it about his legs. On the fifth day a slight rain fell, and by lying down on their backs, they caught some of it in their mouths. At noon McDonald stood up and saw a vessel about six miles to windward. By their united efforts the two men tore up a piece of the planking of the raft, This they split up and succeeded in fastening McDonald's shirt to it. In about an hour they saw the vessel which was close hauled, fall off two or three points, and they knew that she had seen them. Soon afterwards she came up and proved to be the barque "Leandro" Captain Guadalich. The men were taken on board and landed at Boston, and, both being Englishmen, they were received by the British Consul there and subsequently sent to New York.

TERRIBLE SUFFERING OF TWO SHIPWRECKED SEAMEN.

ENCOUNTER WITH A GHOST Nᴿ BRIERLEY HILL

ENCOUNTER WITH A GHOST

The following letter was addressed to the Editor of the Brierly Hill and Stourbridge Advertiser:

"Perhaps you will afford me space to give a short narrative of an adventure which occurred while crossing Whittington Common which people who are acquainted with the locality know is a lonely place at night. I had been to Kinver and remained rather longer than I intended and about half past eleven passed Whittington Inn. In two minutes or so I was in the solitude of the Common. With the silence around me I was on my guard in case I should be surprised or set upon by some desperate character but let no one suppose I was oppressed by the silence or solitariness. No such thing—I was enjoying the solitariness and drinking delight from the wondrous beauty and calmness of the scene and jogging along at something like three miles an hour. From the time of leaving Kinver I had not met a single soul but at this moment just as I was about to ascend a hill—I observed a figure approaching.

Its manner of approach struck me as strange, it appeared rather to glide than to walk, but I accounted for this by the softness of the ground which prevented me hearing the footfalls. At this moment the moon was overshadowed and a comparative darkness fell upon the scene. There however, the figure still stood, and I could see it plainly although the moon was obscured. I demanded why I was thus stopped but there was no answer and I made an attempt to pass on one side. I was far from feeling assured that I could force a passage and raising my stick with all my force aimed a blow at the unwelcome visitor. My blow was well aimed but my stick passed straight through what ought to have been a head. The swing made me stumble and I heard a low chuckling laugh. The figure extended a long arm and I was pressed gently but irresistibly down until I was laid upon my back on the wayside. A cold sweat broke out and the phantom continued to stand about a yard away. I could see it with perfect distinction as the cloud had passed from the moon and she was again pouring a silver stream over everything around.

At last day began to break and as the first ray gilded the clouds on the eastern horizon the phantom lifted up

91

both its arms over its shadowy head, uttered once again its mocking chuckle, and disappeared.

I felt immediate deliverance and reached home in a complete state of exhaustion, mental and physical. I can only say that I never get drunk and was perfectly sober. Moreover, no dreams visit the bestial sleep of a drunkard. Others will say that I must be a timid man and that my imagination played me a trick. To this I would say I am not of a timorous nature and my health was never better at the time. How to account for the adventure I cannot tell but I shall not forget the experience of that horrible night.''

APPALLING DISCOVERY OF TWO SKELETONS IN A THEATRE

We are in receipt of a sketch forwarded by Don Montaria, of Villarina, Spain, which forms the subject of our engraving.

The facts of the case, as briefly detailed by our correspondent, are as follows:—

It appears that the timbers in the roof of the theatre were in a state of decay—and the workmen engaged in repairing the building were surprised and alarmed upon removing the boards that ran round the upper part of the edifice, at finding the ghastly forms of two persons who were locked together in a last deadly embrace. Upon closer examination the workmen found a large Spanish knife buried deep in the chest of one of the figures, the handle of which was still grasped by the fleshless hand of the other figure, in whose neck the broken blade of another weapon was found. It was evident from the position of the combatants that a deadly struggle had taken place in which the lives of both men had been sacrificed. The place in which they were found was a narrow passage between the boards and outer brickwork scarcely two feet in width and there is every reason to suppose that these remains which were but skeletons had been concealed for very many years. It is stated that a carpenter belonging to the establishment, suddenly disappeared some fifteen or sixteen years ago, and the conclusion is that one of the skeletons may be that of the missing man. The figures were in an upright position when discovered, the clothes they had on being literally "shreds and patches."

SINGULAR ATTEMPT AT SUICIDE

SINGULAR ATTEMPT AT SUICIDE

A few days ago a most extraordinary attempt at suicide was made at Newstadt by a workman named Brunheld. It appears that the man in question has for some months past been subject to most extraordinary delusions, which latterly were of so remarkable a character as to occasion some doubts about his sanity. On Thursday groans were heard proceeding from the upper story of an empty house, and for a long time the neighbours were at a loss to understand which some attributed to supernatural causes. On proceeding to the rear of the house it was discovered that the unfortunate man had made a futile attempt to crucify himself.

He had constructed a rude cross which he fastened firmly with ropes to an upright support and the window sill. Having completed his task he suspended himself by means of a rope round his shoulders and under his armpits. While thus suspended he drove a nail into his left wrist, thus fastening it to the wooden cross. This caused him such agony that it is possible he could not proceed with his task. His sufferings must have been fearful.

By the time he was released he had lapsed into insensibility. The poor fellow has been pronounced mad and has been sent to an asylum. Those in attendance on him say that his recovery is doubtful.

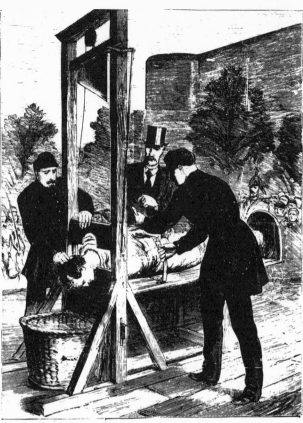

EXECUTION OF TROPPMANN
BY GUILLOTINE

A more than ordinary interest has been evinced in Paris, respecting the final act of the law being carried out in Troppmann's case. His appeal to the Court of Cassation having been rejected, his last resource was to petition for grace to the Emperor. A correspondent to one of the morning papers says: A natural anxiety is felt in England to know how this phenomenal assassin will bear himself on the scaffold, and how the spectators will look on—whether with sympathy for the miscreant on account of his fate, or with an unaltered repulsion. Something more than a morbid curiosity is engaged; there are social problems in action in the crowd, from which lessons may be gathered. It was a necessity, therefore, to be present when the execution took place, but how to ascertain when it would take place? That was the question.

At midnight generally, the horrid redly painted guillotine is taken out of the store, where it is laid up in ordinary near the Roquette prison, and hammered into position in front of the gate. At half-past twelve, accordingly, I drove down to the place with an Irish friend, who had volunteered to keep me company, and who, I must do him the justice to say, kept me in an interesting chat suited to the occasion into the bargain. My friend is well up on executions and tells me interesting anecdotes of how criminals are done to death in various countries. In the Grand Duchy of Baden they are beheaded by the sword (two prisoners are at present lying under that sentence); at Vienna they are carted out of the Spinnerin-am-Kreutz, beyond the city walls and "decently" hanged; in Spain the garrotte is employed—my friend is enthusiastic "it's the neatest system known." But nowhere, in his

opinion outside of Ireland, is that genuine fortitude on the threshold of eternity to be noticed which develops itself by the delivery of a dying speech. These speeches are invariably on the same model. If the condemned is innocent (as sometimes unfortunately will happen) he "knows no more of the murder than the babe unborn;" if guilty, it was cardplaying, night-walking and bad company brought him to his present condition. Thus my companion talks as we rattle along to the sordid outlying district of the town, close by the cemetery of Pere la Chaise, where the prisoner under capital sentence lies.

As we approach the place, the curious in twos and threes, can be seen on the footpaths walking smartly in the same direction, and a hoarse cry can be heard at intervals. We leave the cab at the corner by the open space between the prison of the

Rocquette and that of the Jeunes Detenus exactly opposite. The weather has cleared up and a silver moon shines clearly down from a sea of blue on the spectators who have flocked thus early to secure places in the "theatre of the poor". About five hundred persons of the lower classes are present, chattering, smoking and moving about. The grouping is picturesque, brawny ouvriers in blue blouses eagerly gossiping in knots, boys running playfully hither and thither, shouting as boys will, soldiers of the line out for a night's leave, an old woman with a coffee can crying out her cheap refreshment, cabs in the distance but the chief element of the picturesque is wanting. Like most crowds of its kind it is noisy. Can Troppmann hear those cries and laughs? What is he thinking of? Even he can only guess the date fixed for the expiation of his crime by straining his ear to catch the sounds from without. What is the subject of his meditations. Hood has sang of Eugene Aram that

"Murderers walk the earth
between the curse of Cain
With crimson clouds before their
eyes
And flames about their brain
For blood has left upon their
souls
Its everlasting stain!"

But he is a murderer apart—his thoughts as far as we can learn are never repentent. He is wrapped up in the craven fear of the punishment that awaits him, the only remnant of humanity in his bosom is an affection for his mother.

The people have come prepared for a bivouac; they carry flasks in their pockets and have their trousers stuffed into their boots. As the guillotine should have been turned out by this hour if the execution were intended for morning, I made up my mind that I had had my journey for nothing and drove of weary enough, but satisfied that I had done my duty.

The crowd I am told continued on the place throughout the hours of the night and on the raw of the morning when it was still stationed at the prison gate awaiting its prey.

PARIS Wednesday. Troppmann was executed this morning at 7 o'clock precisely. He walked up the steps of the scaffold quickly and in an agitated manner. The crowd assembled to witness the execution was immense.

SHOCKING
MURDER AND SUICIDE

About seven o'clock on Wednesday evening a most premeditated murder was committed in a field near the Shuttlingfields Farm, Walton-le-Dale, about four miles from Preston.

The victim of the outrage has just turned her eighteenth year and was the daughter of Mr. Brindle the farmer. The murderer and suicide Charles Hamer, was about twenty years old. Both were employed at the Mill of Mr. Brown and for about three years Hamer and the girl had been on intimate terms. Recently she had received from Hamer a letter in which he asked her to meet him after leaving work in St. Martin's field. On leaving the mill she mentioned the letter to her sister and stated she wanted nothing more to do with him. The sisters travelled together as far as St. Martin's field, the murdered one remaining with Hamer and the other sister continuing home, Subsequently she was found in St. Martin's Field with three fearful wounds in her throat from which blood flowed copiously. The poor girl was conveyed home and everything done to preserve her life, but fruitlessly, as she expired in a very short while.

The Police in the district of Brindle presently found the wretched murderer Hamer suspended from a tree by a rope about two miles from the scene of his crime.

SHOCKING MURDER & SUICIDE

Strange intruder in a lady's bedroom

On Thursday night last week an incident of somewhat novel nature took place in the town of Wellington. Mrs. Beauchamp, a young and charming widow, when about to retire, was alarmed at hearing some strange sound in her sleeping chamber. Being a woman possessed of great courage and presence of mind, she flew to an adjoining apartment (which was but recently her husband's dressing room) and took therefrom a pistol. Armed with this weapon she returned and at once proceeded to look under the bed to see if anyone was concealed. To her surprise a young man of prepossessing appearance and having anything but the appearance of a robber, was there discovered. He crept out of his hiding place and murmured a few broken sentences. Mrs. Beauchamp, however, did not care to hold parley with the stranger; she presented the pistol at his head whereupon he begged for mercy. The household was aroused and the intruder was about to be given into custody, but some explanation took place from which it appeared that the erratic individual in question had no felonious intention. According to his own account he was a victim to the tender passion, being, in point of fact, over head and ears in love with the housemaid. The story told by the Gay Lothario appears to have gained credit with the mistress, who did not give the fellow into custody, but contented herself with discharging her maid.

MURDEROUS ASSAULT

On Monday last a desperate dispute took place at Newcastle between a workman and a foreman. From words they came to blows and while on the ground the life of the foreman hung on a thread. His brutal antagonist armed himself with a large stone, which he was about to hurl at the head of his prostrate foe, when several hands belonging to the same works rushed forward and secured the offender. The cause of the quarrel was some trade dispute. How the matter will end it is not possible to say at present.

EXTRAORDINARY SCENE AT A WEDDING

A most extraordinary scene took place on Monday morning at St. Jude's Church, Newtown. The solemnisation of matrimony between a man and a woman was being performed. The happy pair, as it is customary to call them, stood in front of the altar. The clergyman proceeded to read the marriage service. All of a sudden there was some commotion in church which was followed by several peals of laughter. A woman with a baby in her arms, and two children by her side, suddenly presented herself at the altar; whereupon addressing herself to the clergyman, she declared that the marriage ceremony must not be proceeded with. "And why not?" said the bridegroom's best man.

"Because a man in this country cannot legally marry two women", answered the newcomer. "I am his wife and these are his three children". A faint scream escaped the lips of the bride who then fainted away. The consternation and terror depicted on the countenance of the faithless husband it would be utterly impossible to convey to the reader by description.

Of course the marriage was not proceeded with as there could be little doubt as to the truth of the woman's statement. The clergyman closed the book. The bride was borne by her friends to the carriage in waiting for her and the whole party broke up in "admired confusion". It is rumoured that legal proceedings will be taken by the parents of the young lady who was so cruelly victimised by a man whose only object was to become possessed of her property.

EXTRAORDINARY-SCENE AT a -WEDDING.

ANOTHER EXTRAORDINARY SCENE AT A WEDDING

A French paper relates a thrilling scene which lately occurred in a Parisian mairie. A couple presented themselves to be married, the bride about eighteen years of age and possessed of considerable personal attractions; the bridegroom an extremely small man aged forty-five. When the ceremony was concluded, the door of the hall was burst open, and a woman of gigantic stature accompanied by a thin damsel of fifteen, burst into the room and elbowed her way through the semi-circle of guests. "Wretch, scoundrel, thief!" she cried, addressing the husband, who turned as white as a sheet; "this is how you leave me in the lurch, who have sighed during fifteen years for the day when I might call myself your wife!" Saying this she seized the unhappy man by the collar and jerked him up under her left arm as though he were a crush-hat, taking no notice of his struggles. She addressed the mayor in a voice of thunder "do I arrive too late?" "The marriage is concluded" replied the mayor "and I request you to release M. Augustin and to retire."

"Not," said the giantess, "without giving his deserts to the villain who leaves me with this girl here." "No, no, that girl is not mine," howled the little man. He had better have remained silent. **The giantess frantically raised him in the air and whirled him round her head. "Repeat what you have said," she said "this child who is as like you as one pea is another—is she yours or not?" M. Augustin did not open his mouth. His executioner then seized his nose in her left hand and wrung it violently. About this time, two of the guests, moved by the entreaties of the bride, attempted to interfere, but the enraged woman, using the bridegroom as a weapon and brandishing him at arm's length, charged her opponents with such fury, that she put them speedily to flight.**

"Call the police, cried the mayor". "You need not give yourself the trouble" hoarsely ejaculated the giantess; "I will let go the rascal of my own accord. Here my beauty" addressing the bride, "is your little bit of a man" I have not broken him. We have no further business here. Follow me, Babtistine," and so saying she flung her victim at the feet of two agents of police, who at that moment appeared at the door "I go," she added; "but let him ever appear before me on his wife's arm, and I will take him between my thumb and forefinger and make but one mouthful of him."

This little incident cast quite a gloom over the assembled guests, and no one dared even to pick the fainting bridegroom from the floor until the last echo of the heavy footsteps of the injured fair one had died away in the distance, when they raised him to his feet, and in solemn silence took their departure.

SHOCKING CRUELTY

At Middleton on Thursday last, a woman named Jane Rowstock, made a furious attack upon her step-daughter, whom she struck with her clenched fist, knocked down, and then kicked most unmercifully. Had it not been for the intervention of the neighbours the probability is that the poor girl would have been murdered.

MURDEROUS ATTACK ON A WOMAN AT WHITNEY

On Thursday last week, at Whitney, Edward Roberts, gardener, about thirty-five years of age, was sent to the Oxford County gaol on the charge of attempting to murder a young woman named Ann Meyrick, by slicing off a part of the back of her head with an axe. The prisoner lodged with the girl's mother, and he had proposed marriage to Ann and had been refused. Last week he discovered that she preferred a younger man, and in his passion he swore that he would murder her. On Sunday morning while the mother was at church, and the girl was wiping up some water that she had spilt on the floor, Roberts, without a word to her, got up from his seat near the fire, went into the back place, and returned with an axe concealed behind him. **Holding the handle with both hands, he aimed at the back of Meyrick's head; and such was the force of the blow that he cut off a slice—scalp, bone and brain.** He then coolly put the axe back in its place and walked towards the police station to give himself up, expressing not the slightest contrition or regret. Somewhat to the surprise of the medical men, the girl has survived; but they consider that there is but small hope of her living.

MURDEROUS ATTACK ON A WOMAN AT WITNEY

AWFUL DEATH STRUGGLE

STRANGE DISCOVERY

Our readers will doubtless remember the trouble the Modoc Indians gave our troops in the lava beds. The war is happily now at an end, and all that remains of Modocs are the few prisoners that are at our mercy. A few days ago a party of hunters made an exploring expedition, and paid a visit to the far-famed lava beds. A number of strange sights were presented to their curious gaze, but the most remarkable was that which forms one of our illustrations—the remains of two human beings, fixed and rigid in their last death struggle, which ended in death to both. The bayonet of the one had pierced through the body of the other; but the soldier who defended himself with the last-named weapon, was stabbed to the heart by the Modoc Indian, whom he vainly strove to capture.

THE DEATH STRUGGLE

SHOCKING MURDER
✠ NEAR GRIMSBY ✠
SUICIDE OF THE MURDERER

A shocking domestic tragedy was enacted on Saturday at Stallingborough near Grimsby. Christopher Leedham, a brick manufacturer, at Stallingborough, five miles westward of Grimsby, is a man in humble circumstances, aged sixty-five. Some twenty years ago he was left a widower with five children and afterwards married a young woman who was his junior by many years, and who has now fallen a victim to his

eldest son, George Leedham, aged thirty-six. The son when working as a labourer in a cake mill at Hull a few months ago, met with an accident which caused an internal injury of the nature of a rupture. This injury, from which he had only partially recovered, led to a depression of his spirits and produced great irritability of temperament, and he had become almost uncontrollable in the last few days. On Saturday, about half past

twelve o'clock, Mrs. Leedham and her husband (who had just entered and was reading a newspaper), the unhappy son George and his half brother Elijah aged seven years were waiting for the mother who was about to serve up a rice pudding, when George who stood by the table on her left side, began to eat the pudding out of the dish with a butcher's knife. The stepmother requested him not to do so, but to sit

down and to have some of the pudding on a plate. **Simply ejaculating "I shan't" he struck a backward blow with the knife which entered the lower part of the right side of the unfortunate woman's neck just about the breastbone, to a depth of three inches and penetrated the jugular vein. He withdrew the knife, threw it on the floor and rushed out of the house towards the brick pond and jumped into the water.**

He was quickly followed by a brother-in-law aged seventeen, and a labourer named Jackson, who succeeded in dragging him out. The youth then left them and hurried home to ascertain the fate of his mother, who had staggered into the next cottage, fallen down and expired immediately. Meanwhile a struggle ensued between the murderer who was determined on self destruction, and Jackson, in which Leedham proved the stronger, and as Jackson clung to him to prevent him carrying out his intention, he was dragged into the pond, and to preserve himself was compelled to release his

hold, and the murderer succeeded in drowning himself. The deceased woman had ever behaved in the most kind and feeling manner towards her invalid stepson and had the previous day taken home for him from Grimsby market, brandy, wine, and confectionery.

On Monday, Mr. Marris, Coroner for the district presided over a Jury

at the "Green Man Inn" Stallingborough, to inquire into the circumstances above described; and also upon the body of George Leedham, aged thirty-six, who after having inflicted the fatal wound upon his stepmother, drowned himself in the brick pond. The verdict in both cases was Homicide by Leedham whilst in a fit of insanity.

MURDER AND MUTILATION OF A WOMAN

A fearful crime has been committed by a man named James Bradworth, a ship's carpenter, residing within a few leagues of this town. It appears that Bradworth has been living with a native woman for sometime past. It is rumoured that he recently formed a fresh connection; anyway, the unhappy creature with whom he co-habited has been cruelly murdered, after

which her inhuman paramour deliberately proceeded to cut up the body, portions of which he placed in a trunk. Whilst thus engaged he was arrested, and it is said, the weight of evidence against him is conclusive, and that his guilt is beyond all question. For the credit of our countrymen we could have wished this otherwise.

HORRIBLE CANNIBALISM

The New York papers publish a telegram from Kingston, that a Negro woman, of highly respectable character in the community, has been arrested on a charge of cannibalism. The accusation alleges that she has killed and eaten no fewer than twenty-six children, whom she had inveigled into her house. On a cursory perusal the natural impulse would be to consider the story an impudent falsehood. Highly improbable as this shocking intelligence may be, it is just and barely possible. Is Obeahism quite dead in Jamaica? It has been stated that "Vaudouxism" still lingers among the natives of Louisiana; and as regards Jamaica, a careful search through the Parliamentary Blue Books would reveal many extraordinary cases in which evidence was given of the monstrous orgies of Obeah, at which a calabash filled with rum and human brains was a standing dish. It would be worth the while of Mr. Arthur Helps to trace the parallelism existing between African Obeah and the ghastly human sacrifices offered to the Mexican gods described in his Life of Cortes.

POOR BILLET
THE WEAVER
STARVED
TO
DEATH

We have had within the last few days several reports of melancholy cases of death from want reported in the public papers. It is sad to think that men and women should die from starvation in a Christian country, which is perhaps the richest in the world. The sad details in connection with the poor, worn-out weaver, so well depicted by our artist, are as follows:

William Billet was a Weaver of

Bethnal Green. According to the evidence given over his dead body, before the Coroner, William Billet had been trying, for several months past, to live upon such a share as fell to his lot of two shillings a week, received half in bread and half in specie. He died last Tuesday and his

death acquaints us with the miserable details of his life. The jury went to visit the corpse in the small and wretched room where he lived at Anchor Street, Bethnal Green, with his wife and a daughter whose husband was dead. His widow narrated to the Court how he came to leave work in such an abrupt manner. The trio of husband, wife and daughter-in-law had been out of employment for a long time. Eliza Hinkley the daughter in law earned 3/- a week, making trimmings, which paid for the apartment.

On Tuesday, he tottered to the loom from his bed and endeavoured to fix the warp and woof. The experiment had, however, been pushed too far and the poor weaver fell forward on his threads. His wife ran to him and caught him in her arms. "I can't do the work" he cried, "it is too heavy for me" and then without more words he sank forth on his wife's bosum and expired forthwith. All this, we must sadly allow is nothing very remark- able. Belgravia must have silk robes and Bethnal Green must spin them, and when the glossy fabric is manufactured the worm that made it dies. This is an affair of natural history, and long ago accepted as part of the dispensations of Providence.

Meanwhile, before Billet is billeted upon the last universal union, where there is no rent to pay, he measured for us that "distance between Belgravia and Bethnal Green" of which Mr. Bright lately spoke. We have

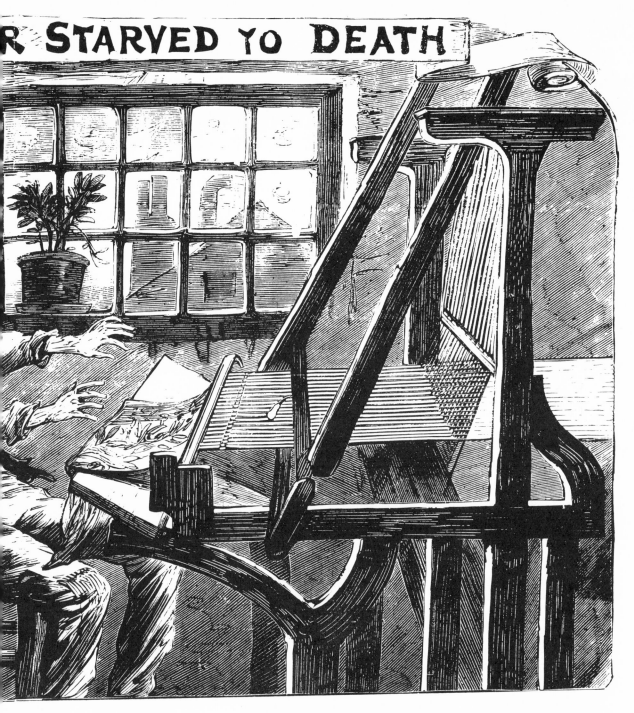

fished him up from the bottom of that vast social ocean, the top so bright with sunshine and gold and the bottom so dark and so cheerless.

Nobody will ever wear that last pattern of Billet's; he did not keep contact to supply beauty and fashion with a "lovely article" at five shillings the week! The "silver cord" of his own life was worn out, and his poor old hands had flung the shuttle too often for the threadbare warp and woof of his frame to stand.

JEALOUSY AND REVENGE IN HIGH LIFE

A melancholy and fatal termination to a drama in real life took place a few days ago at a well known hotel at Coldiz, Upper Saxony. Mr. Mainwaring, an English gentleman of considerable wealth and influence, with high family connections, was suddenly hurried into eternity while slumbering in one of the bedrooms of the hotel. A pistol was levelled and discharged at the illfated gentleman by a woman who claimed him as her

JEALOUSY & REVENGE-TRAGEDY IN HIGH LIFE

husband and indeed from all that has been gathered from the time of our going to press, there can be little doubt that this statement is correct.

About a fortnight ago the victim of this tragedy engaged a suite of apartments at the hotel where he met his death. He had for his companion a young and beautiful female, who assumed his name and passed as his wife. Everybody appears to have been under the impression that the parties in question were a newly married pair on their honeymoon. Letters were received by the gentleman, the postmark on which was Ferrybridge, Yorks. All went on as merry as a marriage bell until the fatal night when the closing scene of this tragedy was enacted. A day or two before this there was a fresh arrival at the hotel. An English lady travelling incognito engaged two rooms on the same floor as those occupied by Mr. Mainwaring and his frail partner. After the two had retired to bed Mrs. Mainwaring, who had evidently matured her deep laid scheme of vengeance, crept stealthily along the passage leading to her husband's bed chamber and entered the sleeping chamber of the guilty pair. She beheld her husband and his beauteous partner. **Without a moment's hesitation she levelled the deadly weapon and fired. The ball passed through Mr. Mainwaring's head and death was almost simultaneous. The fierce, vindictive woman who had only too well carried out her fell purpose was of course arrested but on the following morning she was found to be dead.**

She had contrived to conceal poison about her person, which she must have swallowed soon after her incarceration as the doctors were unanimous in their opinion that she had been dead some hours.

SHOCKING TRAGEDY IN SOHO

A shocking tragedy has taken place in Soho. It appears that six years ago a Frenchman named M. Victor Hasmard Leon Loynon, took apartments upon the second floor of No. 27, Great Pulteney Street, Golden Square, Soho. He was a married man aged thirty years of age and resided with Marie Victoire Leontine Elizabeth Loynon who was some seven years his junior. They lived happily together. His income was £300 a year, which he received from a Parisian firm for watching their interests in London. His wife was entitled to the possession of some house property which had been left to her in Paris. While living in Great Pulteney Street they had a family of four children. Two of their offspring died three months ago and M. Loynon felt deeply the loss he had sustained. Since that time he had been in a very despondent state of mind. On Friday afternoon he left his lodging for the purpose of purchasing a French newspaper. About three o'clock in the afternoon he returned to the house with the paper in his hand. It was then observed that he appeared much depressed. He said that he had first ascertained that the house of his employers in Paris had been destroyed by the German bombardment and that his wife's house property had also been destroyed. He then went up into the room and sat down and whenever he was spoken to he replied in a most melancholy manner.

At half past eight o'clock in the evening his wife proceeded to put her little son aged three years to bed. Just after she had placed the boy upon the bed, her husband entered the room with a double barrelled pistol. She perceiving that he was excited, attempted to rush from the room. While she was doing so he fired at her and shot her through the left jaw. The bullet penetrated her brain and she fell dead on the floor. The murderer rushed from the room and in his hurry he let the pistol fall by the dead body of his wife. He then took another pistol from his side coat pocket. He pulled the trigger and the bullet went through his heart. He died immediately.

Miss Clarke, a young lady of eighteen, living in the house, hearing the report of the pistol shot ran upstairs and was horrified by discovering the corpses of the Frenchman and his wife lying in two small pools of blood. She called in the police, who caused the little boy and the baby aged four months, to be taken to the workhouse

On Saturday the grandmother of the unfortunate children arrived in London and she applied to the workhouse authorities, and removed the children from under their care. The excitement in the neighbourhood is intense and large crowds congregated on Monday in the vicinity of the house where the lamentable tragedy took place.

The Frenchman was a man of middle height and dark complexion. His wife was fair and good looking. Her husband was always very jealous of her. He often said that if ever

misfortune overtook them she should never be loved by another. On the afternoon of the murder she was in high spirits, and was playing merrily with the children.

Another account says that Mr. Hoght, the surgeon, who examined the bodies, and the Inspector of Police, gave it as his opinion that the wife committed suicide by firing off a pistol into her mouth, and that her husband killed himself by shooting himself through the heart. It is supposed that the wife first killed herself, and immediately after a report of the firing of a pistol was heard a fall was noticed in the back room of the first floor and that was followed by another report and a fall in the front room. The deceased had resided in the house for about four years and in the coat pocket of the man was found a letter written to his mother in law, asking her to take charge of his two children, who are now in St. James's workhouse, having been taken there by the relieving overseer.

DREADFUL MURDER AT A BANK

The cashier of the Northern Bank at Newtonstewart, County Tyrone, Ireland, has been murdered, and the bank robbed of its cash, the unfortunate man having been discovered shortly after four o'clock on Thursday afternoon, lying beside the open safe where the cash was kept, his skull having been beaten in, and a box which should have contained £1,600 lying empty beside him.

No trace has yet been discovered which can lead to the detection of the murderer, but every effort is being made to find him out.

Further details of this atrocious murder have now come to hand, from which it appears that a customer was in the Bank transacting business at about three o'clock in the afternoon, and was the last person except the murderer who saw Mr. Glass alive. The murder was not discovered until a quarter past four o'clock, when a servant-maid in the bank came downstairs to see the time through the office door, and when looking in she saw a quantity of blood on the floor and becoming frightened ran out for a neighbour who returned with her. The two opened the door and proceeding to the office found the body extended on the floor, outside the counter. The face was turned downward with the feet toward the door. The mutilation caused to the head was horrible in the extreme, and displayed the utmost possible brutality. From the appearance of the wounds they had all been struck from behind, suddenly and unawares. Strange to say, though all the notes were taken out of the cash box, a quantity of gold was left behind.

A BARON'S CRUELTY TO HIS WIFE

The Paris Tribunals have had before them a very painful case for conjugal separation which tells strongly in favour of M. Naquet's divorce campaign, and partially against marriage with a deceased wife's sister. The parties belong to the highest French society and possess one of the largest fortunes in Europe, being no other than Baron and Baroness Seilliere. The action for separation is brought by the wife on the ground of cruelty and calumny and the husband retorts by accusing the complainant of adultery and other offences.

The Baron's first wife was an elder sister of the present one and died in 1861 leaving two small daughters. The Baron thought he could give his children no better stepmother than their young aunt who had always shown them great affection. She brought no great dower with her but was very beautiful and belonged to a noble family. The hopes for a happy union, however, were short lived as the Baron showed himself to be hasty, violent and brutal. Several times at the very beginning of their matrimonial career the Baron locked his bedroom door and made his wife wait on the stairs for admittance. In 1872 he rushed into his wife's room where she was trying on a corset and kicked a large mirror to pieces.

He now becomes jealous of a young relation of his wife whom he alleges to have lived along with her for whole months and to have laced her corset, to have drunk in the same glass and to have smoked the same pipe. In 1878 in Paris he charged his wife with having poisoned him, knocked her down, kicked and cuffed her, and threatened her life. There are more such shocking charges enumerated against M. Seilliere, and not denied by his counsel. But we have dwelt long enough on this prolonged martyrdom of a wife, who has gone through so much, and is not yet thirty.

A BARON'S CRUELTY TO HIS WIFE.

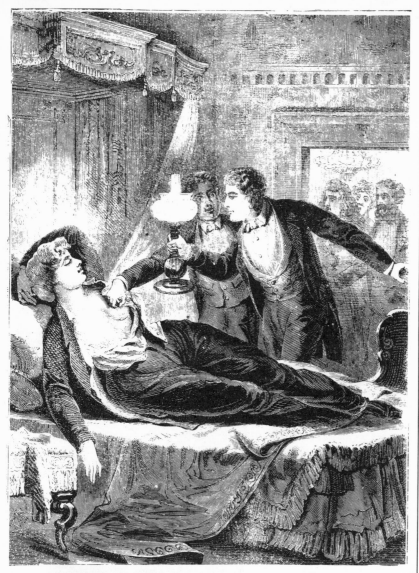

STRANGE DISCOVERY
A Woman dressed in Male Attire

On Monday night, a discovery of a somewhat novel and exceptional nature took place at the house of a gentleman named Bickerstaff, who resides in the neighbourhood of Hadley. It appears that a number of friends were assembled at the house in question where a concert was given, the performers both vocal and instrumental consisting entirely of amateurs. The concert was proceeded by a ball which was very numerously attended, so much so indeed as to cause some confusion and depression to the weaker portion of its attendants. A young man, at least so he was supposed to be, danced with a variety of partners, albeit many present remarked his effeminate appearance, not suspecting at the time the real state of the case. Later in the evening the young man turned suddenly pale. He was observed to gasp for breath. In a minute or so after this he fainted away. He was borne from the ballroom by Mr. Bickerstaff's son and nephew, who placed him on a bed in one of the adjacent apartments. Restoratives were applied without avail.

A doctor was sent for, when a strange discovery took place. The necktie and collar of the patient were removed, the waistcoat unbuttoned, when to the astonishment of those present, the stranger was discovered to be of the fairer sex.

Of course enquiries were immediately set on foot to ascertain who had introduced the disguised female, who was personally unknown to Mr. Bickerstaff's family. The gentleman who brought her assured all present that he was under the impression that she was of the male sex, and that he made her acquaintance on board a steamer which runs from Hamburg to this country. This is all the information that has at present reached us, but it is rumoured that an affair of the heart led the young lady to adopt the disguise she assumed. The circumstance has occasioned no inconsiderable amount of excitement in the neighbourhood, and doubtless in the course of a few days more facts will be known.

TERRIBLE DISCOVERY OF A SKELETON

The Continental papers report an extraordinary discovery of human remains which were found in the portion of an old house at Bardewick, Lower Saxony. The facts of the case are brief but significant enough. They are as follows:

Some workmen were engaged upon building several houses on the outskirts of the town of Bardewick. The houses in the course of erection are close to a small building, which is said to have formed at a very early date a portion of a monastery or convent. Of late years it has been used as a chapel. While engaged upon digging the foundation of one of the houses in question, the workmen came upon a subterranean chamber abutting out from what is now called the chapel. The owner of the ground was communicated with and orders were given to remove the brickwork to make room for the new erection. This was soon accomplished, whereupon some thick oak pannelling was revealed. This the carpenters proceeded to take down when, **to their surprise and horror, they discovered an elegantly furnished apartment, and the remains of what appeared to have been a woman seated at a table in an antique chair. Although clothed, with head resting on its elbow, the body was literally a skeleton. On the table there were several articles —a plate, dish, knife and fork, jug, candlestick, snuff box, etc.**

Scientific men, who have visited the chamber with its ghastly occupant, appear to think from the furniture, clothes, and apparel of the remains,

TERRIBLE·DISCOVERY·OF·A·SKELETON

that the remnant of mortality within the chamber must have had life and existence as far back as three, or it might be four centuries. How she met with her death, and how it came to pass she was left like one asleep in a Glastonbury chair, must, we fear, forever remain a mystery.

LIFE AND DEATH OF A WORK GIRL

Mr. J. Humphrey, Coroner for Middlesex, held an inquest in Brick-lane, Spitalfields, on the body of a poor work girl named Ellen Chatfield, who was found dead in her room on the morning of the 11th ult. Two leading facts of the case as deposed by the several witnesses led but to one conclusion, namely, that the deceased, struggling against a hopeless poverty—and worn out by almost ceaseless toil—had swallowed a powerful narcotic either to drown her sorrows or else to end her existence.

The first witness examined was Jane Laslett, who appeared to be a very decent, well-behaved young woman, who resided in the same house as deceased, who was her friend. At about twenty minutes to twelve on Thursday night she (witness) went into Chatfield's room. She was hard at work and appeared to be very much depressed. She had told witness a fortnight ago, that, driven to the most miserable straits through poverty, she (deceased) had been compelled to pledge some goods belonging to her employer (deceased was a shop worker). She however observed at the same time that she should work hard and redeem the goods—she did work hard, early and late. Witness had observed that her health had very much declined of late. On Thursday night she looked worse than usual. Witness endeavoured to prevail upon her to go to bed. She promised to do so but a light was observed burning in her room when she (witness) retired to rest. How long she remained at work it was not possible to say as all the other lodgers in the house were asleep in their respective rooms. On the Friday morning following, Mrs. Wheatley, the landlady of the house was so surprised at not finding Ellen Chatfield stirring about as usual. An hour or two passed away when at length Mrs. Wheatley came into witnesses' room, and declared it to be her opinion that "something had happened" to Ellen Chatfield. The witness, the landlady, and several of the lodgers entered the room and found the deceased lying on the bed. She was dressed and appeared to be quite dead.

Dr. Harwood said he was told by one of the lodgers that a woman was lying dead in the house kept by Mrs. Wheatley; he made a post-mortem examination, and there could be no doubt as to the cause of death, which resulted from an overdose of Laudanum—but whether this had been purposely or accidentally taken he (Dr. Harwood) would not undertake to say. The witness Jane Laslett was recalled, and stated in reply to the foreman of the jury that Ellen Chatfield had been accustomed to take small doses of laudanum for some internal complaint.

The jury returned a verdict of death by laudanum accidentally swallowed by deceased. **The melancholy end of the miserable girl Chatfield is one of the very many instances of the poorly paid workwomen in the metropolis and our provincial towns—poor creatures who "sew with a double thread a shroud as well as a shirt."**

MIDNIGHT ATTACK AT ST. ALBANS

On Sunday morning, considerable excitement prevailed in the town of St. Albans, in consequence of a report that a murderous assault and robbery had been committed at the Crown Public House, Holywell Hill, by the landlord and his wife during the night, the victim being a gentleman from London, who had attended Mr. Mather's sale of bloodstock on Saturday last and who had money to the amount of £300 in his possession.

The case came up for hearing before the Borough magistrates at 6 o'clock on Tuesday evening, when the Court was beseiged by a great number of persons seeking admission.

The Prosecutor, who was allowed to be seated whilst giving his evidence, deposed as follows:—

"I am the landlord of the Fox & Hounds, Tottenham Court Road, of which house I am the proprietor. I came down to St. Albans on Friday last to attend Mr. Mather's sale of stock on Saturday. I took up my quarters at the Pea Hen Inn where I placed my horse and trap. On leaving I called at a Public House which I have since ascertained to be the Crown, intending to wait for the next down train. I had something to drink and treated the landlord and his wife and other people at the bar. The male prisoner said you can have a bed here. He knew what I was about. I went to bed and both prisoners showed me to the bedroom. I took my clothes off with the exception of my trousers and shirt. I put my waistcoat containing £300 in notes on the side of my bed nearest the window. Previous to that I took my gold watch and chain out of my pocket and placed it under the bed on the other side next to the door. **I went to sleep and was awakened by seeing a man with a lighted candle in his hand leaning over me, and he immediately struck me a violent blow on the head. The female prisoner was also standing behind the male prisoner. Directly he struck me I scrambled out on the other side of the bed. The male** **prisoner came round the bottom of the bed and a desperate struggle commenced between us. I continued to call "Murder" all this time and when I turned away he bit me violently on the arm. Having extracted myself I got the man completely to the ground. When his wife called out the prisoner had just thrown me and had fallen on the top of me. I have marks on my throat now. He had just succeeded in getting his hand on my throat when the policeman came.**

I found my money and felt for my watch but could not find it. I said "where's my watch" and the prisoner handed it to one of the policemen. While I was there the prisoner came to the Station. They made no charge against me but the male prisoner stated they wished to make a statement to the Superintendent. A great crowd assembled outside the Court in order to get a sight of the prisoners as they were conveyed to gaol.

◆▬◆▬◆

113

AN ENCOUNTER WITH A GHOST

On Saturday evening a company of young men were in conversation about the man Crookes, who had committed suicide a few days before by hanging himself, and a bet was made by one of the party that he dared not go and touch the tree where the fatal act had taken place any time between eleven and twelve o'clock at night. At the time appointed he made his way to the spot, inspired with all the courage necessary for his errand, care being taken that a second person had been despatched before him in the character of a ghost.

On his arrival the youth found the mysterious citizen of another world there guarding the sacred tree, dressed in white and having on his head a human skull, inside which a lighted candle was burning. Nothing daunted the valorous hero marched boldly up to the tree, and on attempting to touch it, its spiritual guard dealt him a blow with a stick and threw him down. Upon this his courage began somewhat to give way, and, on rising in a state of great trepidation, he assumed a devotional attitude and raising his hands he exclaimed "Oh, spirit, I conjure thee, harm me not; although thy body is dead I know thy soul still liveth".

Having partially rallied from the first encounter he made a second attempt to touch the tree; he was again repulsed and another blow dealt him across the arm.

The second round seemed to have the effect of renewing his courage, and determined to test his antagonist as to whether he was a spiritual or a corporal visitor, the plucky adventurer made the fence near, and, while in the act of drawing a hedge-stake, the ghost appeared close behind him and threw him against the thorns and briars. Having extricated himself he was again thrown on the ground and kept down until midnight was turned and so lost the wager. When released he scampered down the fields to Dronfield at a furious rate, shrieking and screaming until he reached home.

Horrible Discovery of a Skeleton

The Continental papers furnish us with an account of an appalling discovery that has been but recently made on the confines of the town of Bosario. The bare facts reported are as follows:

Some workmen were engaged in building a new wing to a palatial edifice. While digging the foundations they came upon a mass of brickwork, which formed a series of arches. The style of the architecture of these, together with the materials used in their construction, proved them to be of great antiquity—they belonged, without doubt, to an extensive building of the middle ages. Father Anselmo, a Catholic priest residing at Bosario, hearing of the discovery, hastened at once, in company with several others, to make a careful inspection of the mass of subterranean brickwork. A door leading to one of the vaults was at length forced open by the workmen. The priest and his companions entered. On a stone couch they observed, with feelings of surprise and horror, the ghastly remains of a female; nothing was left but the fleshless skeleton, which was however clothed in the habiliments of a nun. The figure was resting in a half recumbent position.

Father Anselmo, who is a learned antiquary, asserted most positively that the buildings they were inspecting formed the basement, or more properly speaking, the subterranean vaults of a Convent, which was in existence as late as the early part of the present century. Who was the unhappy woman whose skeleton was

HORRIBLE DISCOVERY—THE SKELETON OF A NUN

brought so singularly to light. How came she by her death? Did she carry fast and penance to such an extent as to die of sheer exhaustion—or was she the victim of some harsh, cruel, vindictive, superior. The latter observation seems the most rational one, and if such should have been the case, what offence could the unhappy nun have committed to warrant the infliction of so severe so horrible a punishment?

FIGHT WITH A VULTURE

In a work recently issued by Longmans, a really capital story of the Tyrolean Alps, the heroine is a noble character, full of human tenderness towards the weak and suffering. Such was Elsa Stromminger the only daughter of a rich and influential man. She was called "Elly Vulture" from the following incident of her early life.

Wherever danger was to be incurred there was Elsa to be found. When she was scarcely fourteen a peasant discovered a vulture's nest with a young one, on the face of a rugged rock, whence no one in the village dared to take it. Elsa, however decided she could carry out the

FIGHT WITH A VULTURE

incredible feat and with the help of a rope around her body she was hoisted to the brink of the plateau. She sailed dauntlessly through the air until she reached the young bird who without delay she put under her arm. Then came a rushing through the air and she fought blindly with the infuriated parent vulture who attacked with his sharp beak and claws. Her one thought was "My eyes—I must save my eyes". The battle continued during her ascent but the girl held the young bird firmly and with her face badly bleeding she came to safety. Her father hurried to kiss her because he was touched by her compassion for the helpless creature and felt she had accomplished a heroic feat.

EXTRAORDINARY DISCOVERY OF THE REMAINS OF TWO PERSONS

A most extraordinary discovery has been made in an old mansion situated near Castlebar, Co. Mayo. It appears that Mr. Kennedy, the owner of the house in question, had employed a builder to make some alterations and repairs in the habitation, which is very extensive. In removing a portion of the walls the workmen, much to their astonishment, opened a passage into a large subterranean chamber, with ground arches which had evidently been bricked up, for it was unknown to any of the present occupants of the house. The foreman of the Bricklayers at once hastened to Mr. Partridge, the builder, who accompanied by his men cautiously entered the vault.

The astonishment of all may be better imagined than described when a sight was revealed to them that moved their nerves to wonderment. **The remains of two human beings were made distinctly visible by the lurid glare of the torches they carried. The figures presented a most ghastly appearance being nothing more than skeletons, which were however clothed in the garments of the time of George II. One was stretched on the stones of the vault, while the body of the other rested against the wall in a more recumbent position.** Upon a more careful examination of the premises Mr. Partridge was able to say without hesitation that the vault had been purposely bricked up, as it had doubtless belonged to a set of apartments in the basement of the house. It was his belief that the vault was a sort of "secret chamber" where the occupants of the house in the olden days were accustomed to retire when the place was beseiged. Most old mansions of an early date in this and other countries were furnished with some such apartment.

There have been a number of suggestions made by the inhabitants of the neighbourhood, respecting the two persons found in Mr. Kennedy's mansion, but it is impossible to come to the conclusion that the two human beings were bricked up in the vault

to die a lingering and horrible death, or whether they had been first murdered and placed there for concealment. From their position the former would appear to be the most likely. In any case they must have remained in the gloomy chamber of death for upwards of 100 years. Dr. Swanson made a careful examination of the skeletons and declared that one is that of an adult male about thirty years of age, while the other is evidently that of a lad fifteen or sixteen years of age. **A dark and impenetrable mystery hangs like a funeral pall over this dark deed of a bygone age.**

FEARFUL ENCOUNTER WITH A
BOA CONSTRICTOR

A midnight intruder in the bedroom of an English settler and his wife at Montreal, occasioned the occupants of the apartment so much alarm that for a brief period the power of volition was denied to both. Our readers will not be surprised at this when they learn that a boa constrictor of most gigantic proportions suddenly presented himself in the sleeping chamber of the panic-stricken pair. The facts as furnished by our reporter, are as follows:

A young English farmer named Golding who had but recently married, settled a few months since on some grazing and arable land, situated within an easy ride of Montreal. The house he occupied was a log hut built by a former tenant. Mr. Golding had a brick habitation of a better character in the course of erection. This last he proposed making his home ; but for the present he was constrained to take up his abode in the delapidated hut built by his predecessor. On the night in question he was aroused from his slumbers by a piercing scream from his wife. The cause of alarm was but too painfully evident. A monstrous reptile with open jaws and scintillating eyes was within a foot or two of the bed. Mr. Golding was moved to the utmost extremity of fear and knew not how to act. He and his partner were threatened with instant death which was of a nature too horrible to contemplate. Happily for both, the screams of his wife awoke a man servant who slept in an adjoining apartment. The latter hurried on his clothes, hastened to the door of the room occupied by his master and

FEARFUL ENCOUNTER WITH A BOA CONSTRICTOR

FATAL ACCIDENT ON BOARD SHIP

The barque "Pactullus", of Windsor, Nova Scotia, bound from Newport for Babia, put into Falmouth on Tuesday in consequence of a fatal accident having occurred on Saturday evening. Five of the crew were aloft shortening sail, and three, named John Tyler, Charles Shelley, and Hamsen Holm, who were on the fore-topsail yard, fell, from some unaccountable reason, to the deck. Holm was killed instantaneously, and the other two, who are both seriously injured, were landed there and taken to the Sailors' Home Hospital.

mistress, whereupon the former had sufficient presence of mind to make him acquainted with the facts of the case. The farm servant whose name is John Brightling, after arming himself with a sythe, rushed into the room and with one well directed blow from that formidable weapon, he severed the reptile's head from its body before it had time to effect its deadly purpose.

LUDICROUS SCENE A LADY AND HER PETS

A most ludicrous scene was witnessed by Mr. Beswick, a process-server, in the neighbourhood of Newmarket, on Saturday last. He was instructed to serve notices on the occupants of several houses, one of which is in possession of a Miss Wilkinson, a lady of most eccentric habits. Upon entering the cottage the process-server discovered Miss Wilkinson in the back parlour surrounded by her pets—these being monkeys of every conceivable description. She was nursing and kissing one of the interesting creatures, and did not appear to be at all discomposed at Mr. Beswick's somewhat sudden and unceremonious entrance into her menagerie. She requested him in the coolest manner possible to leave the paper on the table. This done, Mr. Beswick beat a retreat, for it was only by a violent effort that he succeeded in restraining his laughter.

THE DEADLY EMBRACE OF A DEVIL FISH

Early last August a party of Mokaw Indians returning from a visit to their friends (the Songish of Victoria) encamped on the first afternoon out on the beautiful Bay of Metchosen, Vancouver Island. The weather being

THE DEADLY EMBRACE OF A DEVIL FISH.

very fine most of the party went bathing, and among the number a maiden of perhaps eighteen summers, who had accompanied her grandfather on the trip. Desiring seclusion, she went round a point away from the other bathers, and being known as a bold swimmer is supposed to have taken a header into deep water. However taken, it proved to have been a plunge into the arms of death, for when the bathers reassembled round the camp fire the girl was missing, and notwithstanding a deligent search that evening, could not be found. The following morning the party left, but very soon on rounding the first point saw (the water being calm and clear) a human body as if seated on the sandy sea bottom, with what seemed like a flour bag immediately behind it. The natives knew what this meant.

As soon as the canoes got together, two of the most active young men managed with daggers so to disable the monster (for it was a gigantic devil-fish) that the octopus with its victim were brought to the surface. The foregoing facts have been conveyed to our informant by an intelligent and respectable half-breed

woman from Metchosen, who saw the body of the girl with some of the prehensiles of the molusc still adhering to it. She compared the head of the octopus in size to that of a fifty pound flour sack full; said the tentacles were twelve in number, of different sizes, and the largest about the circumference of a man's arm.

Extraordinary Scene at a Wedding

On Saturday morning a marriage was appointed to take place at St. Benet's, Paul's Wharf, between a man and a young woman employed in the neighbourhood. The bridegroom, it is stated, had previously paid his addresses to another young woman and deceived her. She, in the company of her friends, took up their position in the Church, and when the bridal party were preparing to quit the building, assailed them so vigorously that a body of police were sent. Rotten eggs and other missiles were freely thrown, and sometime elapsed before the "happy couple" could escape. A mob of at least five or six hundred persons assembled.

FEARFUL ADVENT

FEARFUL ADVENTURE WITH A SHARK

The natives of Rockaway were recently considerably amused by the antics of a party of rustics from the vicinity of New York, who had come down to the beach to spend a week in aquatic sports. At the time of the incident of which we write, the party, consisting of several ladies and gentlemen, engaged a boat and started out on a fishing excursion, intending to return to the shore and astonish the oldest inhabitants by bringing with them a cargo of blue fish. But as the sequel shows, the laugh was on the side of the "salts" and the rustics were the victims. After patiently waiting for a nibble, one of the females of the party felt something on her hook, and tugging away, the hook was soon visible with a large fish on it.

In the excitement of the moment the girl frantically endeavoured to pull in the fish, but in her efforts she was thrown overboard. The excitement now became intense and the appearance of a shark making towards the young lady increased the alarm. A thrill of horror ran through those in the boat. The women screamed and the men turned pale with fright. The danger became imminent; the shark neared its intended victim.

Not a moment was to be lost. A young man, to whom the female in the water was engaged, plunged in to save her, if possible, and, if not, to perish with her. One of the gentlemen in the boat who happened to have a revolver in his possession, had the presence of mind to fire at the finny monster, who at once made off, meanwhile, the young man had seized hold of his intended, and in a few moments more both were hauled into the boat by their friends and companions.

E WITH A SHARK

EXTRAORDINARY COLLECTION OF CATS

The bench of magistrates at Lewes Petty Sessions on Tuesday were called upon to decide a somewhat extraordinary case. Information was laid by an inspector of nuisances to the Newhaven Board of Guardians, against Mr. Robert Dennis Chantreli, a gentleman also residing at Rottingdean, a small village upon the sea coast, calling upon him to abate a nuisance which existed on his premises in consequence of a large number of cats and dogs and other animals, including a fox and a goat, being kept there so as to be injurious to health. The complainant stated that he was requested by the Newhaven Board of Guardians to inspect the premises and to report thereon. He did so on the 9th instant.

He first visited the garden and there noticed about thirty cats running about loose, two dead cats, and the skeletons of some. From the garden he went to the defendant's kitchen, and there discovered a similar number of the feline race, making themselves very comfortable on chairs and before the fire. A stable or outhouse was next inspected and here between forty and fifty cats were found, some loose and some in cages. In this place raw meat was found laying about in all directions, and was being very demurely gnawed by many of the pussies.

In a yard adjoining the inspector saw upwards of twenty dogs, a fox, a goat, turkeys, geese, ducks and fowls of every description. He next

paid a visit to a house in the defendant's occupation; and attached to his residence. On going upstairs he found all the doors shut, but they were immediately opened and he was ushered into the presence of another nationality of cats. These were in a disgusting condition and on descending to the lower regions he was greeted with the same scene, cats without number, all in an unhealthy state and exceedingly dirty. The total number of cats he would estimate at about 100 to 200. The animals did not really belong to the defendant but were the property of a young lady by whom the defendant was accompanied, who was an artist and resided with the defendant. The defendant was her guardian and had purchased the large premises now occupied in order that she might have her models of animal creation continually before her eyes; in fact she had established a sort of asylum for cats, in consequence of the large number she saw lying dead upon the beach, and even offered premiums to anyone who would bring any animals of the feline species to her city of refuge.

After brief consultation the bench had decided to order the defendant to abate the nuisance in three days, and if a second complaint was made defendant would be ordered to remove them altogether.

A MAN CRUCIFYING HIMSELF

A most remarkable and extraordinary circumstance has taken place in France; indeed the details are of a nature, that, were they not well authenticated, they might be deemed incredible. The following brief account has reached us:— A working stove-fitter of Chateau Thierry, aged about forty, a married man and the father of a family, was found a few days back in his garret, lying on a cross which he had himself constructed out of old rafters, and to which he had actually nailed his two feet and one of his hands. He was removed to the hospital.

A MAN CRUCIFYING HIMSELF

FEARFUL CLIFF ADVENTURE

A scene of a most terrible description was witnessed by a number of persons who were passing over the Jura Mountains. The account given by an eye-witness is as follows: A party of English excursionists were climbing up one of the mountains in question. All of a sudden two persons, a man and a woman, were seen to fall over a precipice. Whether they slipped or part of the earth had given way has not been ascertained. Some assert that the lady slipped and was caught hold of by her male companion; who vainly strove to save her; any way the two fell together. A young Frenchman, who was on a jutting piece of rock on the opposite side of the narrow ravine, held out his hand which the lady grabbed as she descended.

As a natural consequence she dragged down the young Frenchman with her, and all three, the two gentlemen and their fair companion—fell into the abyss below. The lady, Miss McKintosh by name, and the Frenchman, M. Zanite, were fortunate enough to fall on a shelving piece of rock below, where they contrived to support themselves by clinging tentatively to some brushwood. Their less fortunate companion was dashed to pieces, so it is presumed, for his body has not yet been recovered. The other two were rescued by some peasants from their perilous position, and are by this time restored to their wonted health. It is said that a mutual attachment has sprung up between the two in consequence of this adventure.

FEARFUL CLIFF-ADVENTURE

A CHILD SAVED BY A DOG

A most remarkable case of watchfulness and sagacity in a dog occurred on Tuesday last within a short distance of Newcastle. The facts are as follows: A little boy named James Alford, who had been playing with some companions some few minutes before, had been left by his playmates for a few minutes, who, out of fun, hid themselves behind the rocks. James Alford who was stretched on a shelving piece of ground, commenced rolling over and over sideways after the approved fashion of children. In a few seconds he approached the edge of a precipice, being at the time, in all probability, unconscious of his danger. A retriever dog, the property of the boy's parents, seemed all of a sudden to awake to a sense of the little fellow's perilous position, for just as he was about to be precipitated over the edge of the precipice, the dog seized him by the dress and held him over the yawning abyss till assistance arrived. And there can be no question about the fact that James Alford owes his life to the sagacity of his dumb companion.

A CHILD SAVED BY A DOG—ASTOUNDING ESCAPE

FATAL ALPINE ACCIDENT.

FATAL ALPINE ACCIDENT

The following are some additional particulars of the unfortunate accident at the Tete Noire Pass:— The accident occurred some distance beyond the hotel, on the road to Chamounix. The party consisted of an English gentleman, Mr. Rivington, of Babbicombe, Torquay, formerly of the firm of Messrs. Rivington, publishers, with his wife and family. They were travelling in two carriages. A horse in the first carriage became restive, kicked over the traces, and upset the carriage over the precipice, which is not very deep at that particular point. The wife was killed, the father received injuries on the body, and had both wrists broken. No injury was sustained by the second carriage. The party were conveyed to the Hotel Chatelard as the nearest to the spot, and a despatch was sent to the British Consul at Geneva, to send the best doctor immediately. He left at once and found that every attention had been paid to the injured by Mr. Manby, a surgeon from Chamounix. The patient is progressing favourably, but several days must elapse before he can be removed to Chamounix, and thence to Geneva.

CHARGE OF THROWING A WOMAN FROM A WINDOW

At the Liverpool Court on Saturday, John F. Lopez, a coloured man, was charged with having thrown his wife Margaret, out of a window, in a house where they lived, on Friday night. They were both quarrelling and shortly after the woman was seen to fall from a window, a distance of thirty-five feet. She lies in a serious condition. The prisoner was remanded.

A shocking double murder and suicide was committed on Monday morning, in the village of Tintwistle, near Glossop some fifteen miles from Manchester. A mother murdered her two children, and then took away her own life. In a cottage in a locality known as the Stocks, a respectable labouring man named James Gregory, his wife, and three children resided and from all our reporter has been able to learn, they lived peacably together. The eldest child was a boy of seven years old, the next a girl aged three, and the youngest an infant only a week old. The eldest and the youngest are the victims of this terrible tragedy.

About a quarter to seven o'clock on Monday morning, the father was awoke by his wife and to his surprise he found her quite dressed in holiday attire. She told him it was time to go to work and as she had been confined only a week ago, and had been out for the first time the day previously, her being dressed did not excite his suspicion. He considered it a sign of her convalescence. About seven o'clock he left the house for his work, he being employed as a ganger upon the Manchester water-works. At the time his little boy, aged seven, and the infant babe were in bed with his wife, the little girl being away for the night at an aunts. The embankment that he was sinking had however been flooded with water, and he was unable to commence his employment. He returned home, and arrived there about half past eight o'clock. He found the front door locked, contrary to custom, for a neighbour who had been engaged to light the fire and prepare the breakfast had been in the house and done her work. The fact of the door being closed excited his suspicions, and he ran round to the rear of the house. The back door also was fastened and he procured a ladder reared it up to the back chamber window, and by this means gained access to the house.

A fearful spectacle met him. The little boy lay on the floor in a pool of blood, with his head almost severed from his body. His neck had a fearful gash, some three inches in length, cut on each side, and although the jugular vein was severed, the windpipe was untouched. The poor little fellow had bled to death and there were traces that he had struggled for life. After

126

the wound had been inflicted the boy had crawled from the bed to the window, and left a bloody trail behind of some three yards in length. The husband naturally suspected that someone had entered the house and murdered the lad, he rushed downstairs and raised a cry of "Murder". The house was searched and in the same bedroom as the boy had been found, the infant child was discovered quite dead, overhead in a pail of water. In the cellar the mother herself was found hung to a beam, quite dead.

It is evident that she first murdered the boy, cutting his throat whilst asleep in bed, with a razor, which she had procured from the room below; had fetched a pail of water upstairs, and thrust the babe head first into it, for on the garments of the child were marks of the mother's bloody fingers. The boy must have been attacked whilst asleep, or he would have proved a formidable antagonist for his mother; he was a stout lad and

she was weak through her confinement. For sometime past she has been in a desponding way, and her recent illness has quite deranged her brain. To this is the tragedy assigned, for it is said that she lived comfortably with her husband.

On Wednesday, Mr. Johnson, the Cheshire coroner, held an inquest at the "Waggon and Horses" Inn on the bodies of Rebecca Gregory, thirty-one; William Gregory aged seven and Nancy Gregory, eight days old.

James Gregory, quarry miner, in the employ of the Manchester Corporation, Tintwistle, said the deceased Rebecca Gregory was his wife. She was thirty-one years of age. The deceased William Henry Gregory, was his son and seven years of age. The deceased Nancy Gregory was his daughter and was eight days old. He went to his work on Monday morning and left his wife in bed with the infant by her side. His little boy was in another bed in the same room. Just before leaving home he said he

would come as usual for breakfast. The little boy was asleep. He returned home at twenty-five minutes to nine, and the door was locked. He knocked several times and received no answer, and got in by the back chamber window. When he lifted the blind, he saw the little boy lying at the far end of the room, on the floor, under the window, and quite dead. He went out and gave an alarm, his brother came, and witness and he went into the cellar and saw his wife hanging from the beam, dead. He did not find the infant then. His wife was attended by Dr. Pomfret. She had been in a low desponding state of mind for eighteen months, but he did not see any difference that morning. A neighbour (Mrs. Marshall) and the deceased's sister attended his wife during the day.

The Coroner: Had she threatened to do this act? Witness: On Sunday she said they all would die together.

THE HOUSE AT TINTWISTLE

BOY SCALDED TO DEATH

THE SCHOOL AT MOTTRAM

DOUBLE MURDER AND SUICIDE IN CHESHIRE

ROMANTIC SUICIDE

Coroner: You took no action? Witness: No, I tried to pass it off as well as I could. By the jury: She awoke him at five o'clock by pulling his whiskers, and she was then dressed. She pulled her boots off and lay down in bed. She was dressed when he left. She did not appear agitated and he noticed nothing in her hand. He did not know when she dressed herself but she had undressed to go to bed. Mr. Pomfret, surgeon, who attended the woman in her confinement, said he last saw her alive on Sunday morning. She was dressed and getting over confinement remarkably well. She had been in a low desponding way for some months. The husband and children had suffered from an attack of fever, and she was continually imagining that something was going to happen.

Coroner: She never gave you any impression of any suicidal intention! Witness: She gave me no suspicion of anything of the kind.

Coroner: There was no suspicion or you would have taken some steps? Witness: No, she seemed perfectly rational.

The Coroner, in summing up, said there was no doubt the two children met their death by the hand of their mother but the Jury would have to say whether she was responsible for her acts. It was very fortunate that the husband was not a victim also, for there could be no doubt that when she was feeling his whiskers in the morning she intended that he should die too.

The Jury returned a verdict that the deceased, Rebecca Gregory, had killed herself and her two children whilst in an unsound state of mind.

⚯

BOY SCALDED TO DEATH

On Wednesday Mr. W. Johnson a Coroner, held an inquiry at Mottram into a case of an extraordinary character. At the Mottram grammar school are four boarders, and it is the custom on Saturday evenings for the boys to wash each other. On Saturday the master Mr. Briggs was in Manchester and the eldest boy in the school Oliver Whittle, aged sixteen, so treated a little fellow of seven, named John Goodall, son of the late Mr. Edward Goodall, Deansgate, Manchester, as to cause the child's death. It appears from the evidence that the servant gave Whittle two gallons of boiling water. Whittle poured this water into the bath and seized Goodall, thrust him into the liquid and held him down.

Goodall screamed and struggled and ultimately got out of the water. He ran round the room in agony, and Whittle again seized him and thrashed him with a hazel stick. Whittle called upon another boy to fetch a strap to bind Goodall's hands, and again thrust the poor lad into the water. He then washed him rubbing the skin off the poor little fellow's body "by handfuls".

The injured lad at length got out of the water, partially dressed himself and ran downstairs into the kitchen. The servants put oil on his wounds and he went to bed but he did not sleep. The next morning Mr. Briggs noticed that Goodall was very pale and seemed in great pain and he examined him and sent for Dr. Pomfret. The child's skin was found to hang about him in shreds. Dr. Pomfret stated that the injuries were of the severest possible character, indeed the flesh had been in a manner killed and had this not been the case the lad must have suffered dreadfully. Goodall gradually became worse and died on Monday morning. Whittle's mother lives in the neighbourhood of Preston.

The Coroner said that though Whittle had doubtless no felonious intent in putting the boy into the water, yet it was a piece of most flagrant cruelty, for he must have known from the lad's screams that he was in great agony.

The Jury returned a verdict of Manslaughter against Whittle, who was committed for trial at the assizes his bail, however, being accepted.

ROMANTIC SUICIDE

On Saturday afternoon Mr. Donaldson, deputy coroner for Middlesex opened separate inquiries at the "Bell and Hare", High Road, Tottenham, upon the bodies of two Frenchmen, who committed suicide under very singular circumstances. In investigation in the first case was with reference to the death of Francois Joseph. Last Wednesday night he went to the "Lord Palmerston" tavern, West Green, Tottenham, and inquired for a bed. He could not however be accommodated there but obtained what he required in the neighbourhood. About five o'clock the next evening he went to Mount Pleasant fields, a rural spot lying between the main road, Tottenham and Hornsey Gate, and was seen by some children to throw away his papers. He then climbed into a tree, placed a rope round his neck and threw himself off, falling about four feet. A boy who had seen the transaction informed a cowman who was in the adjoining field and he hurried to the spot and cut the man down.

The second enquiry was with reference to the death of a Frenchman, at present unknown, who was found lying dead, with a beautifully-finished small revolver grasped in his hand, on the marshes near Page's Lock, Tottenham, on Friday evening last. Information was given to the Police and Mr. Hall, surgeon was called. He went to the spot and found that death had been caused by a bullet passing just under the right ear into the brain. Judging from his clothing he was in a superior social position, but he had apparently removed all means of identification. He was somewhat over thirty years of age, about five feet six inches high, and wore a dark moustache.

The Timely Warning

A young Englishman named Cuthbert Wagstaff, had a narrow escape a few evenings ago, at a well known house of public resort in Homburg. It appears that Wagstaff, who is reputed to be immensely rich, has been for some months past on most intimate terms with a girl named Maybrunch. A few weeks ago a quarrel took place between the two, and the young man, her lover, declared that he would never have anything more to say to her. For a brief period the two were estranged; ultimately, however, a

THE TIMELY WARNING

DINING OFF A DEAD HORSE

Herr von Wickede, of the COLOGNE GAZETTE, describing an excursion he made from Belfort to Pontarlier, says "Heaps of forsaken corpses mouldered away among the bushes and in the ditches by the high road. Not far from Montbeliard a doctor and I found eight Frenchmen dead in one house, and already in an advanced state of decomposition. Among them lay a wounded man, still alive, and who cried out in a lamentable voice. We took him out with some difficulty and laid him in the open air. A Prussian grenade had torn his legs below the knee and he had lain in this state for seven days, without water and entangled with the other corpses. He had lived for a week on pieces of biscuit from the pockets of his dead companions and slaked his thirst by drinking great flakes of snow which fell in at the window. **Horseflesh is now the principal food of the inhabitants of the country and I have myself seen a bevy of famished women throw themselves upon a dead horse like a pack of wolves, and, tearing it with all sorts of instruments, swallow morsels quite raw.**

ATTEMPTED MURDER AND SUICIDE

Considerable sensation was caused in Chesterfield on Saturday morning by the rumour that a person named Richard Lee, a clerk (and for some time engaged in that position at the Chesterfield Barracks) had murdered his daughter and committed suicide. On reaching the scene shortly after the occurrence we found the result was scarcely so bad as had been represented. For some time Lee had been jealous of his wife, and when under the influence of drink he had shown his feelings on this matter by being guilty of violent behaviour. He formerly lived with his wife and her daughter in a cottage situated in Mill-street, belonging to Mr. Fidler. We say her daughter because she was born before Lee married the mother, her father being a gentleman engaged in the drapery trade at the present time at Sheffield. About six months

reconciliation took place. The pair met, it is supposed accidentally. They betook themselves to the house already alluded to. Wine was ordered and while Wagstaff was raising the glass to his lips, **he was surprised and horrified at seeing a female's hand holding a paper over the partition which divided his own from the next compartment, on which was written "Beware of Poison".** His female companion, meanwhile, was watching him with the eyes of a lynx. The young man made some excuse, said he did not like the wine, rose from his seat suddenly and affecting to see a friend in the distance, walked leisurely to the further end of the room. When he returned, the girl Maybrunch had affected her escape, and has not since been heard of. A chemical analysis of the wine was afterwards made, and it was found to contain arsenic. The girl who gave the timely warning has been handsomely recompensed by young Wagstaff, who esteems himself especially fortunate in escaping with his life in so miraculous a manner.

DREADFUL DEATH FALLING OVER A CLIFF

An inquest has been held at Skinburness on the body of Edward Wilson. Deceased was driving a horse and cart along the highway on the coast of the Solway Firth, and owing to the darkness of the night he had missed his way, and driven the horse and cart on to a piece of green ground lying between the road and the sea brow. This piece of ground was only eleven yards in breadth, and the poor fellow had driven the horse to the very edge of a cliff, which at this point is ten feet high, and horse, cart and driver went crash over on to the beach below. When discovered, about two hours afterwards, Wilson was lying underneath the upturned cart with his neck broken and quite dead. The horse was so much injured that it had to be at once destroyed. Verdict "Accidental Death".

ago Lee went home and used threatening language to his wife, and she applied for a summons against him and he was brought before the borough magistrates. The evidence was clear although Lee made some allusion to his wife's conduct, and reproached her with being guilty of immorality. The Mayor ordered him to enter into his own recognizance of £20, and to find two sureties for a similar amount to keep the peace for six months. The recognizance not being forthcoming he was conveyed to the County Gaol at Derby, where he remained several weeks, when a relation and a tradesman of the town entered into the required bonds and he was liberated.

On his return to Chesterfield he found his wife had taken up her abode in another house, and in consequence of his threats she refused to live with him any longer. He obtained employment for a few weeks and for the past two months he had not worked. His wife and her daughter a short time ago, went to lodge at a house situated near the railway at the back of Eyre-

street, belonging to a man named Thomas Metcalf, who is employed at Mr. Clayton's tanyard. Since she has lived there he has repeatedly visited the house, and asked to again live with his wife, but she has always refused to receive him. On Friday night his feelings appear to have got to their highest pitch, and armed with a shoemaker's knife he hid himself in a privy at the back of the house and watched for the departure of Metcalf. At six o'clock in the morning Metcalf went to the tanyard, which is situated about 200 yards off, leaving Mrs. Lee engaged in blackleading the front room fireplace and the daughter in bed. As soon as Metcalf was out of sight he carefully opened the front door and got to the side of his wife before she was aware of his presence. He said he was determined to stay with her upon which she told him to leave the house, informing him she wished to have nothing to do with him. He then seized her and commenced beating her. She screamed

for assistance and the daughter who it sixteen years of age came downstairs. Lee was then in the act of pulling the shoemaker's knife out of his pocket and the girl succeeded in releasing her mother from his grasp and she made her escape. He then seized the daughter and inflicted a wound across her throat about three inches in length severing the outward vessels, but luckily not injuring any of the main arteries. He was about fo renew the attack when she had a fearful struggle with him in which she received a deep cut across the hand and after that she ran screaming across the yard, Lee rushing upstairs.

Mr. Brown, who lives next door, hearing the noise, went into the back yard and saw the girl standing in an almost fainting state, the blood flowing freely from the wound in her neck. He carried her into Mr. Birchall's house and Metcalf was at once sent for. He (Metcalf) at once went upstairs and found Lee lying on his belly on the floor between the

bedstead and the window in the front room, his head lying in a pool of blood. Mr. Bluett, surgeon, was sent for and in a very short time he was on the spot. Lee was placed on the bed and it was found that he had first cut his throat from ear to ear, and then made another stab at the windpipe, inflicting another gash about three inches long. A large piece of flesh was left hanging from his throat. All the outside veins were severed, and two of the jugular veins were cut, the carotid arteries being laid bare. The wounds were at once stitched up, also the daughter's. The latter is not in a dangerous state and may soon recover, but Lee has jabbed his throat in such a dangerous manner that doubts are entertained as to his recovery. A policeman was left in charge of him to see he did not complete the attempt to destroy himself. A great number of persons have already visited the scene of the murderous outrage.

REVOLTING CRUELTY TO A DOG AND CAT

At the County Police Court for the Leicester Division, on Saturday, William, alias "Nutty" Miles, a poultry dealer, was charged with brutally ill-treating a dog and cat at Rearsby, on the 30th ult. This is the most revolting case of cruelty to dumb animals, perhaps, ever recorded; and Mr. Haxby who appeared to prosecute on behalf of the Society for the Prevention of Cruelty to Animals, asked that the prisoner might be sent to gaol without the option of a fine. In the first case, the prisoner, who had been to Melton market, on returning, stopped at the "Horse and Groom Inn" Rearsby. He was much the worse for Liquor. After being there a short while, he picked up a small dog belonging to Thomas Keeling, of Queensborough, which was lying on the hearth, and threw it on the fire which was a very large one and burning brightly. The dog was got off the fire and it appeared to suffer much. When remonstrated with he said "he would burn all such chaney faced ——— all to bits." Defendant subsequently picked up a kitten, which he hid behind his back until the landlord had left the room. He then went to the boiler, which was full of boiling water, lifted up the lid, put the cat in and held the lid down. When taken out, which was as soon as

possible, the cat was quite dead, the fur and flesh peeling off. The magistrates sentenced him to be imprisoned for six months with hard labour (three months in each case) without the option of a fine.

Appalling Carriage Accident on Hackney Marshes

ROASTING A DOG ALIVE.

On Thursday evening a sad occurrence happened at Hackney Marshes which has resulted in a fatal consequence to one if not more persons. It appears that towards evening a phaeton, in which was a gentleman, his wife and three children, was being driven by the former along the road through the Marshes leading from Homerton to Stratford. When nearing the bridge which crossed the canal, the horse took fright from some cause not apparent, the driver losing all control of the animal which appeared to be very high spirited. It dashed along at a fearful rate and could not be brought up. The lady and the children in the phaeton were of course frightened, but kept their places, little thinking of the dreadful result which was to follow.

Within a short time of the horse dashing off it was noticed by many persons who were unable to arrest its progress, that it was making towards the canal and rushing over the bank and the whole party were precipitated into the water which at this spot is of considerable depth. A scene of the wildest excitement immediately ensued; and several persons rushing to the canal, the gentleman, his wife and two of the children were with difficulty rescued. The other child was not extricated until life was extinct and another one in an almost hopeless condition.

On being taken out of the water the unfortunate persons were conveyed to the Victoria Tavern adjoining, where they received every attention. The carriage was completely destroyed and the horse so much injured that it had to be killed.

ROASTING A DOG ALIVE

At the Chapel-en-le-Frith Sessions, James Thorpe and Daniel Mann, aged seventeen years respectively, were charged with cruelly ill-treating and torturing a dog, the property of Mr. Boden of New Mills, on the 8th ult. The Society for the Prevention of Cruelty to Animals represented by Mr. Richard Ward, prosecuted. Frederick Kenyon took with him to Thorpe Farm a dog of Mr. Boden's. He was with it in the kitchen and had it on his knee, when a youth named Bagshaw came and knocked it down. Mann then took it to another room and

DEAD.— VILLANOUS CRUELTY.

when he (witness) next saw it it was running down the brow on fire. On reaching home its master did what he could to relieve it suffering but had to have it destroyed. The magistrates consulted and convicted respondents in the full penalty of 40s. and costs.

DEAD
Villainous Cruelty

Our engraving is a representation of a sad incident in connection with the stocks, which were at one time used most extensively in this and other countries. The circumstances to which we refer occurred some years ago in Staffordshire. A tramp named William Pitcairn, weary and footsore, rested at a small roadside house. Some young men who chanced to be there treated him to several pints of ale. Poor Pitcairn, it appeared, had not broken

his fast for several hours, and as a natural consequence he became half stupified with the beer. While in this state his tormentors led him to the stocks, in which they firmly fixed his feet. This done they hung his faithful dog on one of the supports, and left both dog and master to their fate.

In the morning poor Pitcairn was found dead by some of the neighbours, a coroner's inquest sat on the body and the jury returned a Verdict of "Died from want and exposure". The inhuman wretches who had placed the tramp in the stocks escaped with a mere nominal punishment.

TWO PRISONERS
FLOGGED AT NEWGATE

There was a scene in Newgate on Saturday norning which would, we think, have an excellent effect on "roughs" and garotters could they have been witness of the exhibition and seen its effect. At 10 o'clock the Sheriffs arrived and about half a dozen representatives of the Press; the Governor Mr. Jonas, and the surgeon. On one side stood a black set of old looking stocks with holes

for wrists; the bottom being an enclosed box. There was no delay; Mr. Sheriff Bennett stood watch in hand, close to him a stoutish, short grey man, in what is known as a cardigan jacket, and two warders ushered in the first prisoner, Bernard Regan, a stout muscular young man with a low type of countenance, guilty of helping to inveigle a man up a court where the poor wretch was nearly kicked to death, robbed and left with one eye hanging out upon his cheek. Regan had been sentenced to thirty lashes, seven years penal servitude and seven years police supervision. The warders assisted him to prepare. There was a good deal of the wild beast about his aspect but he remained very cool and in a few seconds the cross arms of the stocks were opened and closed upon his wrists and the box like lower part opened admitting him and enclosing the lower part of his body.

Samuel Lily was the second offender upon whom sentence was to be carried out, a younger more boyish looking fellow. He stood smiling as he stripped off his shirt, evidently holding the operation in contempt, but his thinner, fairer skin, threatened to give place to more suffering as it proved. His punishment was to be but twenty-five lashes for robbery with violence and the same time of imprisonment and supervision as was awarded to his fellow.

The effects on his skin were horrible, the diagonal pink lines glowing scarlet and running into one another till there was a broad scarlet band which quivered and flushed and changed colour, but there was no blood. Twenty-four, twenty-five lashes and then came a loud voice "Stop" and the prisoner was cut loose to walk quietly away from the post. There was nothing in fact, more than what seemed to be wholesome punishment. That it was deserved the account given of the misdeeds fully bears out.

A clergyman flogging a boy

A case heard at Grantham County Petty Sessions has attracted considerable attention from the curious example it gave of the petty tyranny that may be exercised by a country clergyman. It seems that at the village of Ingoldsby, some few miles from Grantham, a couple of boys, one eleven and the other six years old, quarrelled in the churchyard on Saturday week and the biggest lad threw a stone at the little one and made his nose bleed. The mother took her son to the house of the culprit's father, and requested, but not very mildly, that the offender should be punished. The father, one Edward Schofield, did not satisfy her that he would comply with her request, but

A CLERGYMAN FLOGGING A BOY AT GRANTHAM

immediately she was gone he did punish his son. The mother of the injured boy, whose father was in the service of the clergyman as a groom, made a complaint to his employer The Rev. J. H. Hilyard, rector of the village and a county magistrate. The reverend gentleman, who is of very irascible temperament, took up his groom's case very warmly and sending for the local policeman ordered him to fetch the boy Schofield immediately before him. The elder Schofield insisted that he had corrected his son but the reverend gentleman persisted that the boy should be punished before him. The policeman whipped the lad and was instructed by the Rev. Hilyard to ''lay it on harder''. The flogging was still continued but the Rev. Hilyard considering it still too lenient seized the whip and gave the lad a few parting cuts himself.

Schofield took his son to a surgeon who described the boy's back as being a mass of escoriations, there also being an abrasion upon one shoulder.

Mr. Hilyard and the police officer were both charged before the County Bench at Grantham with the assault. The reverend gentleman, although a magistrate, conducted himself in Court in an unseemly and violent manner, for which he was repeatedly corrected. At the close of the case, which lasted nearly four hours, the Chairman announced that they had unanimously agreed the assaults were proved and fined Hilyard £2, and costs, also the policeman 2/6d. and costs.

FEARFUL SCENE
WOMEN TORN TO PIECES

A report of a dreadful scene has reached us from Javat. It appears that a lady who is as rich as she is eccentric has for the last three or four years become a sort of cat fancier; she not only breeds these domestic pets, but has been accustomed to purchase any choice specimen of the feline race that might take her fancy. A few weeks ago a fire broke out in the house of the cat fancier. Two maid servants were despatched to a sort of shed or cage on the basement of the premises to unlock the door of the same and release the cats. The devouring element was by this time in the ascendant, and the cats were in a state bordering upon madness. The moment the door was unlocked they flew at the unfortunate young women, whom they bit and tore most unmercifully. The injuries were of such a serious nature that both have died therefrom.

SCENE ON PLUMSTEAD COMMON.

Scene on Plumstead Common

A large meeting was held at Woolwich on Monday night last week, to celebrate the release of Mr. John De Morgan from Maidstone Gaol. At seven o'clock a crowd of some 2,000 persons assembled in the Arsenal Square, where addresses were delivered by Dr. Baxter Langley, Mr. De Morgan, and others. DeMorgan stated that he should not cease to agitate until they had defeated their opponents, or been themselves worsted by an adverse decision in the High Court of Justice. He was, he said, very comfortable at Maidstone Gaol, where he was treated as a first class misdemeanant, and during the seventeen days of his confinement he received and answered no less than 295 letters.

At eight o'clock a procession was formed round the principal streets of Woolwich and Plumstead. Two bands with torches and banners, accompanied the procession, De Morgan riding at the head in a carriage drawn

...UL SCENE — WOMEN TORN TO PIECES BY CATS

by four greys. Next came a number of waggonettes, containing the most prominent "commoners", and in the rear a cart containing effigies of two gentlemen who had taken a leading part in the prosecution at Maidstone. Immense crowds lined the streets all along the route On arriving at the middle of Plumstead Common, the procession was brought to a stand before a pile of faggots and a gibbet which had been previously erected.

Here the two effigies were hung in chains over a fire until they were consumed. At this time an immense crowd was present, the fifty-five acres of common where the fire took place appearing almost covered with people. The procession moved on to another portion of the Parish where the meeting was brought to a close. A large force of police were held in readiness but their services were not required.

CAPITAL punishments

The series of illustrations upon Capital Punishment will doubtless be found most interesting. The question of punishment in cases of murder cannot be too freely discussed.

Death is the greatest punishment mortals can inflict, beyond this their power does not extend. It was not thought a sufficient punishment simply to take the life of the culprit, but he was put to death by methods the most cruel; made to endure pains the most excruciating, and when the vital spark was extinguished his lifeless

form was insulted and treated with brutality. Such fearful spectacles cannot be viewed by the humane and feeling without horror.

Nevertheless, we do not think it right or consistent that the punishment of death should not be inflicted in "all cases of murder".

HANGING AT TYBURN TREE

It was the custom down to a period of as little as eighty years ago, little more or less, to execute malefactors at this now fashionable locality.

Tyburn was, in fact, the chief and most favourite place of execution in London. It was at the western end of Oxford Street, near to the north-eastern corner of Hyde Park. The gallows appear to have been a prominent erection resting on three posts, hence the name "Tyburn Tree". Wooden galleries were erected nearby for the accommodation of spectators.

THE PUNISHMENT OF THE CORD (CHINA)

The usual capital punishments of China were strangling and beheading. The former is the most common and is decreed against those who are found guilty of crimes which, however capital, are only held in the second rank of atrocity. For instance, all acts of homicide, whether intentional or accidental, every species of fraud committed upon government, the seduction of a woman whether married or single, using abusive language to a parent, plundering or defacing a burial place, robbing with destructive weapons and for wearing pearls.

BEHEADING ON TOWER HILL

Beheading was a military punishment among the Romans. The head of

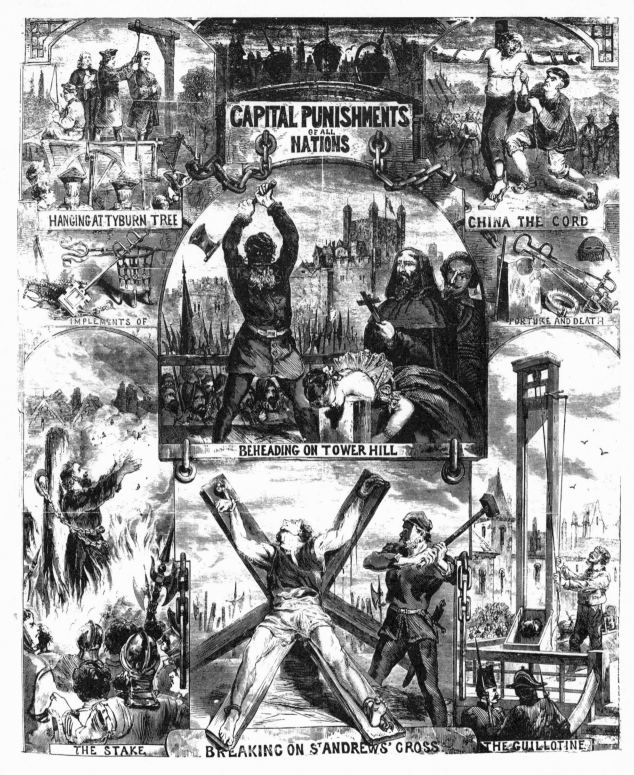

CAPITAL PUNISHMENTS OF ALL NATIONS

HANGING AT TYBURN TREE

IMPLEMENTS OF

BEHEADING ON TOWER HILL

CHINA THE CORD

TORTURE AND DEATH

THE STAKE

BREAKING ON ST ANDREWS' CROSS

THE GUILLOTINE

the culprit was laid on a block placed in a pit dug for the purpose beyond the VALLUM and preparatory to the stroke he was tied to a stake and whipped with cords. In the early ages the blow was given with an axe but in due course of time the sword was made use of.

This mode of capital punishment was first introduced into this country from Normandy, by William the Conqueror in the year 1076, when Waltheof, Earl of Huntingdon, was first so executed.

THE GUILLOTINE

Was invented for the purpose of causing painless and immediate death. Whether it successfully accomplished this desirable object we do not pretend to say. A physician named Joseph Ignatius Guillotin claimed to be the inventor of the deadly instrument named after him.

The Maiden was made use of in this country long before the introduction of the last named into France. The

English mode of decapitation was usually by the block and axe—with one local exception—that of what was called the Halifax Gibbet, which was indeed a perfect Guillotine and had been of old employed in serious cases arising in the adjoining district.

In the forty-nine days in which the guillotine is said to have stood at the Barriere du Trone, it despatched 1,270 persons of both sexes and of all ages and ranks.

BREAKING ON ST. ANDREW'S CROSS

This punishment was similar to the one known as "Breaking on the Wheel". It consisted of breaking the leading joints of the body with a large hammer and concluded with a coup de grace on the head.

BURNING ALIVE

Burning alive was inflicted among the Romans, Jews and other nations, and was countenanced by bulls of the Pope. Many persons have been burned alive as heretics.

CRUELTY TO A DAUGHTER

At Brentford on Tuesday morning last week Thomas Edward, a pensioner from the army, was sentenced to six months' hard labour for ill-treating his daughter Alice, a girl of fourteen years of age, by beating her over the head with a glass bottle and over the body with a broomstick. The poor child's arms were covered with bruises, and one one was an incised wound, caused, she said, by a knife being thrown at her.

SHOCKING MURDER AT NEWCASTLE

On Tuesday last, a woman named Elizabeth Mathewson, living in Blenheim Street, Newcastle, was found dead in bed by a man called Purdy. The woman's forehead was covered by large wounds and presented the appearance of having been smashed in by some blunt instrument. The police were called and they found a coal rake with several spots of blood upon it. They took possession of the house. A doctor examined the body, and gave it as his opinion that the wounds had been inflicted by a blunt instrument. The deceased had in her service a woman named Barbara Sample, who, it was suspected, murdered her mistress. She was apprehended while attempting to enter a friend's house on Wednesday at five a.m. She was taken to the Police Station and there confessed that she had murdered her mistress, and added that she had told her to kill her. She took up a coal rake and struck her several times on the head. The housekeeper is addicted to drink, and her object in murdering the old woman has apparently been to gratify her vicious taste, as the house had been stripped of everything valuable.

When the corpse was discovered the face was quite clean, all the blood having been wiped off it and the bed clothes were neatly turned down. It appears from the coroner's inquest held on Wednesday night, that the prisoner after committing the deed, slept all night on the same bed as the dead body. She had stated that she murdered her mistress on account of their poverty and other things. She took the poison at the request of the old lady and they both agreed to lay down and die. Two letters were found in the room addressed to the deceased's nephew. One of them was as follows: "Sir—It is your aunt's wish for her and I to go out of the world together, for no one knows the poverty she has been in, and I have had to take my own things as well as hers. We are no more when you get this. BARBARA SAMPLE."

An inquest was held on Saturday night in the "Durham Ox" Inn on the body of a married woman named Barbara Sample, who died on the previous day from the effects of poison. Inspector Tunnah was the first witness and he said the body just shown to him was that of Barbara Sample, forty-three years of age, the wife of Mark Sample, a mariner. Mr. George Rowell, assistant surgeon at the Infirmary, next spoke of the

CRUELTY TO A DAUGHTER

reception of the woman into that institution and expressed the belief that she had died from the effects of poison.

The jury returned a verdict to the effect that deceased died from poison administered by her own hand but there was not sufficient evidence to show her state of mind when she administered the drug.

Mark Sample, the husband of the deceased, attended the Infirmary next day and at once identified the body as that of his wife. He stated that they had not been living together for six years in consequence of the woman's drunkenness, and he had shifted his residence to Lynn, in Norfolk, in order to keep out of her way when on land. Although his

vessel had been lying in the Sunderland Dock for three weeks, he asserts that he never heard anything what-

ever of the murder until a woman informed him of it in the theatre on Saturday night.

MYSTERIOUS DEATH AT PENGE

The inquiry respecting the death of Harriet Staunton, which took place under somewhat extraordinary circumstances, was resumed on Saturday morning at the Park Tavern, Penge, by the Coroner for West Kent. The room was filled by the general public to overflowing.

Evidence was given that after her death she was locked in her room without the landlady being informed of her death and a certificate was

obtained from Louis Staunton from Dr. Longrigg under false pretences. Then when the coroner stopped the funeral at a moment's notice by telegram, and ordered a post mortem, the result as proved by five medical gentlemen, and admitted by Mr. Harman, who had been called in by the Stauntons to watch the examination on their behalf, was found to be that the unfortunate woman had been actually starved, and that even the

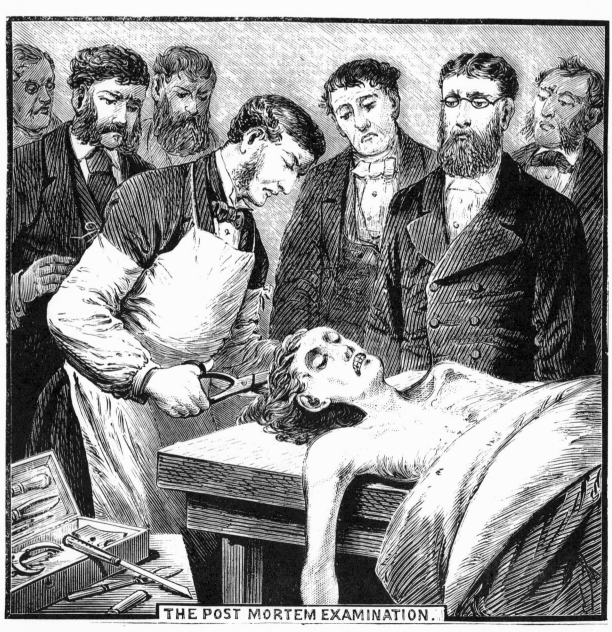

THE POST MORTEM EXAMINATION.

dinners spoken of as being taken by her on Tuesday and Wednesday before death, could not have been eaten. **The deceased was simply skin and bone, looking fifty instead of thirty-five, the stomach, intestines and rectum being perfectly empty, with the exception of what had been forced down her throat on the morning of her death. The medical evidence was clear that the cause of death was long continued starvation. The other symptoms led to the belief that poison had been given to her, and Professor Rodgers and all other doctors expected to find poison from the appearances inside.**

The motive for the death of the woman was clear, for Louis Staunton was living in adultery with Alice Rhodes, and having obtained more than £3,000 from the deceased, and no more being likely to come, the latter was simply a burden upon him, to be got of, when he could if he chose to marry the sister of his brother's wife. He lost nothing by the

deceased's death and gained nothing by her living. It was murder, and nothing else but murder, and not manslaughter, and the jury, if they thought that such was the case, and that the deceased had been neglected with malice aforethought, would return a verdict to that effect.

The jury retired to consider their verdict, and after an absence of twenty minutes returned a verdict of "Wilful murder against Louis Staunton, Patrick Staunton, Elizabeth Staunton, his wife, and Alice Rhodes," and the coroner made out his warrant to them to take their trial at the next assizes.

FATAL FALL FROM A CLIFF AT RAMSGATE

A sad accident happened on the east cliff, St. Lawrence, Ramsgate on the Sea, on Saturday last week, by which a young man named John Peterkin lost his life. He was one of a very large party of excursionists who came down for a day's pleasure by the seaside. It is surmised from his extraordinary conduct that he was partially intoxicated. Towards evening he was observed by the coastguardsman on duty in front of his

station on the cliff with a party of friends, seemingly very hilarious and much inclined to rough play and jokes. About half past five o'clock he was seen to leave his companions and seat himself on the very edge of the cliff with his feet overhanging.

Before there was time to remonstrate with him or restrain him, he raised himself up from his already dizzy and hazardous position, upon his elbows, and was endeavouring

EXTRAORDINARY WIFE MURDER

Three years ago a suit for nullity of marriage was prosecuted by Mrs. Sweet, formerly Miss Watts, of the Globe Hotel. The suit was unsuccessful and after Mr. Sweet had been abroad for a few months he returned and the two settled down together, residing at Clifton Place. They have since September last lived together, apparently on excellent terms. On Wednesday afternoon, however, when they were at home and in their bedroom a quarrel arose originating from his wishing for some pomade for his toilet. Mr. Sweet proposed to send the servant out for some and Mrs. Sweet objected.

THE MURDER.

The servant was sent and on her return found her mistress lying on the floor, fearfully wounded. The husband had run his wife completely through her head with a sword, the weapon entering one temple and coming out at the other. The struggle between them appears to have been a severe one, Mrs. Sweet having received several cuts and gashes across the wrist and arm in vain attempts to defend herself. The body of her dress was also torn open.

The altercation took place at about a quarter past three o'clock and at about five and twenty minutes to four, Mrs. Sweet expired.

On the servant entering the house Mr. Sweet left it, ran to the cabstand at the end of Torrington Place, and ordered the cabman to drive to the Guildhall.

Next morning at the Guildhall, Sylvanus Sweet was examined before the magistrates on a charge of wilful murder.

The morbid and melancholy curi-
The morbid and melancholy curiosity which seizes the public to catch a glimpse of any criminal, or to hear the details of any horrible act, had its effect on Monday morning, for the Guildhall was crowded to suffocation to hear the re-examination of Sweet, for the murder of his wife.

From evidence taken it appears that Sweet committed the crime whilst suffering an epileptic fit. After some further evidence the prisoner was fully committed.

Murderous Assault

On Monday last a desperate dispute took place at Newcastle between a workman and a foreman. From words they came to blows, and while on the ground the life of the foreman hung on a thread. His brutal antagonist armed himself with a large stone, which he was about to hurl at the

---

to draw his body up, resting his weight upon them, when the shattery surface gave way and the unhappy man was precipitated instantaneously to the bathing sands below, a distance of seventy-five feet.

Police-constable Stead who was on duty on the sands, and others went to his assistance, but he was beyond the reach of human aid, his head being crushed by the force of the fall. The remains were taken to the nearest inn "The Elephant and Castle" to await an inquest. The unfortunate deceased was very respectably dressed, and his friends stated that he was a single man, twenty-two years of age, and a confectioner in the employ of Messrs. Hill and Jones of London. The sad affair has caused a great deal of painful excitement in the neighbourhood.

A cold dip

On Friday last week a young man within a short distance from Newport, met with a rather singular accident. It appears that for sometime past he had been courting a young lady, the daughter of an irascible gentleman, who was much averse to the visits of the would be lover. Ultimately an elopement was planned by the lovers. A ladder of ropes was procured, and while holding the same for the lady to ascend, the parlour window was opened and the young man received a severe blow, which sent him headlong into the water butt. The affair has occasioned much mirth in the immediate locality.

head of his prostrate foe, when several hands belonging to the same works rushed forward and secured the offender. The cause of the quarrel was some trade dispute. How the matter will end it is not possible to say at present.

ATTEMPT TO STRANGLE WIFE

On Friday last at Newton, a man named Johnson, in a fit of fury, threw a cord over his wife's head and drew the same tightly round her neck, evidently for the purpose of strangling her. The poor woman struggled desperately and managed to scream loudly for assistance. Luckily her cries were heard and some of the neighbours rushed in and rescued her from her impending fate. The man is said to be suffering from delirium tremens.

FATAL AFFRAY AT A GAMING TABLE

The fatal effects of giving way to passion have been but too painfully and forcibly shown in a fracas which took place in a gaming house at Aix-la-Chapelle, a few nights ago. A dispute suddenly arose between two English gentlemen, who, it appeared had been betting on the game besides staking certain sums on the board. Captain Bainbridge, one of the disputants, made use of most insulting language to a Mr. Rowton. Swords were drawn and to the surprise of those present the disputants were engaged in a deadly conflict.

Before anyone had time or presence of mind enough to separate the combatants, Mr. Rowton's sword passed through the chest of the illfated Captain Bainbridge, who fell to the floor and expired without groan or struggle.

The sister of the dead man, together with several females who were dancing in the ball-room, in close contiguity to the gaming table, rushed in. The scene that followed can be better imagined than described. Mr. Rowton at once gave himself up to the municipal authorities, and it is stated that he is so borne down and in such a low state of mind, that those who have charge of him have deemed it expedient to place a watch on him to prevent him from committing suicide. As a natural consequence this tragic drama in real life has been the theme of conversation for some days past with the visitors to the town in question.

FATAL AFFRAY AT A GAMING TABLE

FATAL ACCIDENT TO AN IMPALEMENT PERFORMANCE

The NEW YORK MERCURY has the following: "Julia Bernard, a vocalist, danseuse, and a very pretty girl, met with a tragic death recently. She was standing against the board whilst an actor was showing his dexterity in hedging her in while hurling knives into the board, Six knives had been stuck between each arm, just above each shoulder and at each side of her head. The aim of the thrower was too low. The knife penetrated the brain and the girl sank down to die. The actor is under arrest."

FATAL ACCIDENT TO AN IMPALEMENT PERFORMANCE

ZAZEL SHOT FROM A GUN

The overflowing audiences throughout the afternoon and evening are to be taken as a test of the growing popularity of the Royal Westminster Aquarium. There can be no doubt as to the success achieved on Easter Monday last, for after two or three o'clock, until the close of the performances, locomotion in the building was a matter of great difficulty. The magnet of the day was unquestionably Zazel, a young and comely female trapezist of the most adventurous order. After some perfectly self possessed gyrations on an almost invisible wire, fixed high up in the Grand Hall, this aerial support is suddenly withdrawn and the artist is found suspended on a trapeze on which she performs some astonishing feats.

Lashed to one of the side galleries was what appeared to be a large cannon into which Zazel was placed. At a given signal the cannon was supposed to be fired, a loud explosion followed by a cloud of smoke, took place, and a moment afterwards the late occupant of the cannon was seen in the vast net below, whence she retired amidst the cheers of the audience.

ZAZEL SHOT FROM A GUN

ATTEMPTED MURDER BY A SON

At the Town Hall, Leicester, on Wednesday, Thomas William Sturges Frisby, twenty-one years of age, was charged with shooting his father Thomas Frisby, a sheriff's officer, with intent to murder him, on the previous night. The prisoner some years back enlisted in the 101st Regiment, but had been bought off by his father. Since his return he had formed the acquaintance of a young woman, who was objected to by his parents, and through this words are said to have ensued between Mr. Frisby and the prisoner, which led to the latter leaving his father's house, in Newarke-street, about seven weeks since, and going to lodge at a Mrs. Collins's. One day last week he went to a public house and enquired if his father was there and on being answered in the negative he replied, "I'll do for the ———— I have a bullet for him;" at the same time taking one

from his waistcoat pocket. On Tuesday afternoon it would seem he went to the parent's house and enquired for his father. He went to the house again at ten o'clock at night, and on his mother coming to the door, he said he wished to see his father. She replied that he had better not as he seemed in liquor and advised him to call another time, but he insisted on having an interview, and, after some altercation, rushed by his mother and ran through the sitting-room, into the kitchen where his father was eating his supper. He at once pulled a pistol from his pocket, and deliberately aimed at his father's head. The shot took effect the charge entering Mr. Frisby's right cheek. The wound bled profusely and is described as of a serious character, although happily it is taking a favourite course. The prisoner was taken into custody about midnight while asleep at his lodgings. On being charged with shooting his father, he replied, "All right; I know all about it;" and on the way to the station he said "I should think the old man had got a basin of soup, that he knocked it over and it must have exploded". Subsequently he enquired "Has he kicked out?" the policeman supposing the inquiry meant "is he dead?", answered "No" upon which the prisoner replied, "It is time he was then". On prisoner arriving at the Police Station he tried to secrete the powder and shot which he had about him by throwing it about the floor, but he was observed by an inspector. In his waistcoat pocket was found more shot and powder—The prisoner was remanded to Monday.

EXTRAORDINARY SUICIDE.

EXTRAORDINARY SUICIDE

One of the most ingenious engines of destruction ever put together, was that of young Pillsbury, at Chelsea, Mass. The machine consisted of two perpendicular pieces of joist about two feet apart and reaching from the floor to the roof of the barn. About six feet from the floor had been adjusted in a piece of wood, a large, sharp axe, so that it moved up and down in a groove. This axe was held in its place by a water pot filled with water, attached to a lever, which in turn was made to support the axe. A hole had been made in the water pot so that when sufficient water had leaked from it to overcome the leverage above, the axe would fall. When all arrangements had been made, the young man got upon his knees, and, putting his head through an aperture made at the bottom, slowly and calmly awaited death. He had previously supplied himself with about two pounds of ether, and while the water was slowly dripping from the pot he placed the ether in his mouth. When found the head was only hanging to the body by a small piece of flesh. **If anyone says the Yankees are not the most ingenious people in the world, and that this quality is not strong even in death, call his attention to Pillsbury's invention.**

BABY FARMING AT BRIXTON

The evidence given in this case before the police magistrate at Lambeth, on Monday (last week) was of a remarkable character. The name of one of the prisoners is Margaret Waters who lives at 4 Frederick Terrace, Brixton, and she was charged with neglecting to provide food and nourishment for the illegitimate child of a Miss Cowen, daughter of the bandmaster of the Royal Irish Volunteers, whereby its life was in danger, Sarah Ellis of 4, Langholme Villas, Brixton, was also charged with being concerned with the first named prisoner for having four infants in her possession, also in an emaciated condition.

Sergeant Ralph of the W. division said: About twenty minutes to one

Murder and Attempted Suicide

An inquest was held on Friday on the body of Reuben Holmes, who was murdered in Beck Lane, Nottingham, on Thursday, by John Buchan. The first witness called was Lucy Buchan, a widow, who said she knew deceased who was in her service as a dyer. He had lived in her shop in Beck Lane and was about fifty-three years of age. Witness was there on Thursday morning as also was the deceased. About half-past nine o'clock her son, John Buchan, came to the shop, and the conversation turned upon money matters. Deceased afterwards said "There is nothing worth living for" and witness's son replied "No there is not". The latter then began to cry and said he was nearly wild. Soon afterwards he asked witness to fetch him some snuff, the witness at that time being engaged in shelling peas. Witness went out for the snuff and on reaching the bottom of the stairs she heard the report of fire-arms twice. **She went back into the house and saw Holmes and her son bleeding. She immediately raised an alarm. The police came and witness then saw a pistol on the floor. She did not know of any disagreement between her son and the deceased. When she went out she left her little boy, the deceased and another little boy seven years of age in the room. No one else went in while she was out. She was not out of the room two minutes. Her son lost his wife about twelve months ago and had since been very despondent.**

Mr. H. Hine, Resident surgeon at the Nottingham Dispensary, said about twenty minutes to eleven on Thursday morning he was sent for to the deceased and found him in a shop in Beck Lane, lying on his back and bleeding profusely from a wound behind the left ear, from which the brain was protruding. He died about three-quarters of an hour afterwards. It appeared like a gun shot wound and would admit the end of the finger. There were marks of gunpowder on the neck. Witness had since opened the head and found the wound extended forward to the right temple, crossing the substance of the brain. He found the bullet lying between the membranes of the brain. It would have been almost impossible for the deceased to have inflicted the wound himself. The inquiry at this point was adjourned—The prisoner, John Buchan, who shot himself, has been removed to the General Hospital; and it is thought possible he will recover.

MURDER AND ATTEMPTED SUICIDE AT NOTTINGHAM

BODY OF A CHILD FOUND UNDER TIMBER | BODY OF A CHILD FOUND UNDER A R^Y ARCH

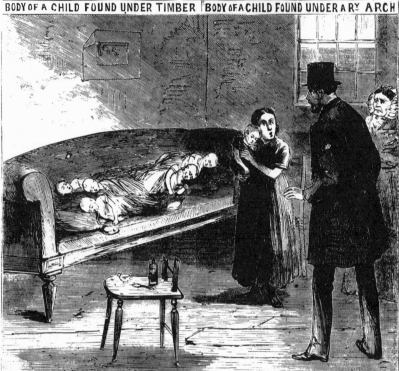

BABY FARMING AT BRIXTON

on the night of Saturday, the 28th May, I saw a four wheeled cab draw up at the front door of 165, Camberwell Road, kept by Mrs. Barton, a mid-wife. I saw an elderly woman get out of the cab, go into the house, and shortly return with a delicate looking young lady, who I thought had been recently confined. I followed the cab and saw the woman get out at Lang-holme Villas, Brixton. I ascertained the young lady's name was Jeannette Tassie Cowen, and that she had been recently delivered of a male child at 164, Camberwell Road. I made enquiries and ascertained that the child had been put out for adoption to a woman named Willis who advertised for infants, but no one knew where she lived or what she was. I saw an advertisement in Lloyd's of June 5th, signed by a Mrs. Oliver, to adopt for £5 to cover every expense. I answered it and made an appointment to meet Mrs. Oliver, which I kept at half past eight at Camberwell New Road, on the 12th June. After seeing her Mrs. Oliver said she had been married fourteen years but had no family—this I have since ascertained to be false. She said her husband was a house decorator and lived at Herne Hill, was well to do and if I entrusted my dear boy to her care, it would be well educated and put to her husband's trade. She seemed very anxious to get a boy and also for me to leave her. I traced her and found she resided at 4, Frederick Terrace, Brixton.

At 9 o'clock on the 11th I went to the house and prisoner Oliver answered the door. I asked her to produce Miss Cowen's child. She said it was not there and that it had been put out to nurse. I went into the kitchen and found several infants, three or four weeks old, all huddled together on a sofa. There were seven male and four female infants. They all lay with bottles by their sides. Mrs. Waters said she was paid so much per week. **Dr. Pope giving evidence said all the children were emaciated and very dirty, they all appeared to have been deprived of food and were in a sadly neglected condition. Evidence was given that Miss Cowen's child was remarkably large and healthy when born. Ann Rowland, a wet nurse, gave evidence showing the shocking condition of the infant of Miss Cowen when brought to her. All the infants with the exception of one, were conveyed in cabs to Lambeth Workhouse pending the remand.**

Since the case was originally before the Court the police have obtained further evidence relating to it of such a character that it appears that the charge will shape itself into wilful murder of several of the infants.

CRUEL TREATMENT OF A GIRL

At Wellingborough Corn Exchange where the Court sat on the 11th of August, an excited crowd gathered for the appearance of a man and a woman named Gent who were charged with assaulting a girl named Lovell. The Gent's live in Barnabus Street and the girl is about thirteen years old. Ellen Lovell gave evidence and stated she was thirteen years old, her mother was dead and her father had gone away. Last Thursday week she was sweeping an upstairs room and accidentally broke a wash-stand. Mrs. Gent hit her several times with her hand and the girl offered to pay for the damage done. Mrs. Gent told Mr. Gent and she was sent upstairs to be flogged. **She removed all her clothes but her chemise and Mr. Gent took a strap striking her across her bare back several times. The blows made marks in several places and these were bleeding. The following morning she was again told to go upstairs for another hiding. She was pushed on to the bed and Mr. Gent again struck her with the strap.**

After hearing all evidence the sentence of the Court was that Gent be imprisoned and kept in hard labour for two years. Eliza Gent was sentenced to one month's imprisonment. The decision was received with applause.

Shocking Cruelty to Children

The Folkestone Express of July 1st, gives the following report of a case which has excited much interest in that locality. On Monday afternoon considerable excitement was created in Queen Street by a woman going to the house No. 35 and demanding a child. The house in question is tenanted by a man named Knight who has two children, but lost his wife about three years ago. For sometime past he has resided at the above address with a Mrs. Upton, the widow of a sea captain and who has one child. The neighbours on either side having heard the screams and cries of the children, considered it high time to interfere and on Monday with the assistance of the Police, gained access to the house.

On four chairs in the back room lay the youngest child Thomas Knight, aged three years, in a state of semi-starvation. The child was in a most filthy state being literally covered with vermin. It was wrapped in a pinafore and was saturated with blood from vermine bites. A neighbour took charge of the child and on being given food it ate ravenously.

Eliza Witnall who lives at No. 28 Queen Street, gave evidence saying: "I have not seen the child for nearly two years until yesterday. Mrs. Upton who calls herself Mrs. Knight was out at the time. When she came home we went in because we heard her ill-treating the children. Mrs. Upton had the child in question under her arm and had the other child by the hair of its head. I asked her to give me the youngest child but she would not do so until its father came home. I took up the child which was in a filthy state and appeared to be starving. The child was almost alive with vermin from head to foot. I washed the child and found its back was covered with

SHOCKING CRUELTY TO CHILDREN

bruises. **In my opinion the child was very much neglected. I know that the defendant has been at work lately".**

The Magistrates having consulted, the Mayor said "Thomas Knight, the Bench consider this is a most serious case. In fact I might say it is the worst case I have had to deal with during my term of office. If this child had died you would have been tried for the crime of manslaughter. The child has suffered from want of proper nourishment and clothing, and such neglect on the part of a father in a Christian country is truly deplorable. You have been earning 28/- a week and therefore had the means to provide it with proper sustenance. It is, therefore, out of the question to say that you had not the means to provide for them".

The Court was crowded during the hearing of the case and during the day the house was literally besieged. In the afternoon a crowd assembled round the house, and after pelting the front of the place with filth and dirt, they effected an entrance by forcing the door off its hinges.

Up to a late hour on Tuesday evening the street was in an uproar and at half past eleven o'clock an effigy of a woman was carried about and ultimately burnt.

A number of women assembled at the Junction station in the hope of seeing the man Knight, but were disappointed as he was taken to Shorncliffe and from thence conveyed by train to Dover.

EXTRAORDINARY SCENE IN THE HOUSE OF A HERMIT

In the village of Brooklyn, North Wales, an eccentric individual has resided for a considerable period. He is the sole occupant of a wretched habitation which, it appears, he never allowed any of the neighbours to visit. In short, he lived so completely secluded, and his habits were so remarkable, that the village folk called him a hermit. Little appears to be known of him with the exception of him being an old man bent beneath of nearly four score years, of very dirty habits, and of so morose and moody a temperament, as to cause him to shun the companionship of any of his fellow creatures. On Thursday last, a report was circulated that the old hermit of Brooklyn was dead, he had not been seen in his accustomed haunts for more than ten days. Notice was given to the police and two active and intelligent officers were despatched by the superintendent to make some enquiries regarding the eccentric person. Upon the officers arriving at the house of the recluse, all was silent as the grave, and the habitation presented the appearance of a deserted place. No answer was returned to the repeated knocks at the front door, around which a number of persons had assembled, in addition to the officer who sought admission. At length, one of the policemen broke open the door, and passing through the narrow passage he entered the front parlour. He and some of the neighbours who had entered with him were perfectly astounded at the scene presented to their astonished gaze. Evan Gwynne, the old hermit, was seated in a chair, surrounded with cats, dogs and monkeys. One of the last named animals was perched on the back of his master's chair and chattered at and menaced the intruders. In addition to this, the cats, which it afterwards appeared were half starved, flew at the policeman and his companions so furiously as to cause a momentary panic. The policeman, however, struck at his feline assailants repeatedly with his staff, and contrived to keep them at a respectful distance.

When the first surprise and alarm were over the facts of the case were ascertained. Evan Gwynne confessed that he had been dangerously ill, but at the same time declared that he was gradually recovering, and did not need the advice or interference of any of his neighbours. All he cared about was the companionship of the animals who formed his strange menagerie; for he was sick of the world and at war with all mankind. It was evident that the poor old man was not in his right senses although he could converse collectedly enough. He was, however, pertinacious in his refusal of all assistance. The policeman returned to the station and made the superintendent acquainted with the strange discovery, and later in the day a doctor paid a visit to Gwynn's cottage and succeeded in persuading him to take some necessary medicine and nourishment. It is rumoured that the old hermit was cheated out of a title and estate in the early part of his life. How far this may be true we are not at present able to determine.

HORRIBLE MURDER
BY TWO WOMEN

A hideous French murder has just ended in a sentence of penal servitude for life against a mother and daughter by the Gers Assize Courts. An old farmer named Parterie gave up a portion of his property to his stepdaughter and her husband on the condition that he should receive a life annuity. Tired of this trifling burden the woman resolved to murder her stepfather. **She began by throwing boiling water over his head while he was asleep, and when he awoke attacked him with a red hot bar of iron. The cause of death would thus have been set down as falling into the fire and being scalded.**

After the failure of this monstrous attempt Madame Parterie, the wife of the victim, helped her daughter to strangle the wretched man. Cartade, the son-in-law, who does not seem to have taken an active part in the crime, was acquitted.

HORRIBLE MURDER BY TWO WOMEN.

Horrible treatment of a nun

A telegram from Cracow has already announced that, in consequence of anonymous information, a judicial commission, assisted by the clergy, forced an entrance into the Carmelite Convent in that town where they found a Nun who had been locked up in a dark, filthy room for twenty-one years. She had been utterly neglected, and was quite naked and half mad. Bishop Galeki, who was present as papal delegate, overwhelmed the Abbess and the Nuns with the most vehement reproaches, asking them whether they were women or furies and thanked the judge charged with the enquiry for his timely and energetic interference. The Confessor of the Convent was at once suspended by the Bishop. As may be imagined this intelligence created the greatest excitement. The people eagerly enquired for further particulars, and these were supplied by the following report in the Vienna press.

On Tuesday, the 20th inst, an anonymous notice apparently written by a female hand, reached the Criminal Court at Cracow, to the effect that in the Convent of the Carmelite barefooted nuns, one of the order named Barbara Ubryk has been forcibly kept in close confinement in a dark cell for a long number of years. The Vice President of the Criminal Court Ritter Von Antoniewicz, immediately laid the information before a Judge of inquiry, who, in company with the public prosecutor repaired to the Bishop von Galecki with the request to permit them to enter the Convent. Herr Von Galecki suggested that the notice might have arisen from a false report and he was not inclined to identify such a horrible deed with the tenets of Christian religion or Church discipline, or even to excuse it. He suggested to the Judge that the notice might have arisen from a false report. In his company and with that of his actuary Kwialkowski and the judicial witnesses, the Judge drove to the Convent.

The latter, which is one of the strictest female Orders, is situated in one of the most beautiful suburbs of Cracow. Thousands of people passed these sombre cloister walls without even suspecting the fearful tragedy being enacted within for twenty-one years.

The Convent was first entered by Father Spital, followed by the members of the judicial commission, to whom the porteress attempted to refuse admission. The judge informed the porteress he had come to see and speak to Nun Barbara Ubryk, which information made a terrible impression on the porteress. The commission, however, thereupon went to the upper corridor, followed by the Nuns, one of whom showed the Judge the cell of Sister Barbara. The cell was situated at the extreme end of the corridor, between the pantry close to the dung-hole and had a walled up window and a double wooden door in which there was a moveable grating through which food was probably handed in. **In a dark infected hole adjoining the sewer sat, or rather cowered on a heap of straw, an entirely naked, totally neglected, half insane woman, who at the unaccustomed view of light, the outer world and human beings, folded her hands and pitifully implored "I am hungry, have pity on me—give me meat and I shall be obedient."**

This hole, for it could hardly be called a chamber, besides containing all kinds of dirt and filth, and a dish of rotten potatoes, was deficient in the slightest decent accommodation. There was nothing, no stove, no bed, no table, no chair and it was neither warmed by a fire nor the rays of the sun. This den the inhuman sisters who call themselves women, spiritual wives, the brides of heaven, had selected as a habitation for one of their own sex and kept her therein in

close confinement for twenty-one years since 1848. For twenty-one years the sisters had daily passed this cell and not one of them thought of taking compassion on this poor outcast prisoner. Half human being, half animal, with a filthy body, knock-kneed legs, hollow cheeks, dirty head, unwashed for years, came a horrible human being forward such as Dante in his wildest imagination was unable to picture.

The Bishop ordered Nun Barbara Ubryk to be brought into a clean cell and there to be dressed and nursed, which the Lady Superior obeyed very reluctantly. When led away, the unhappy Nun asked whether she would be brought back to her grave and when asked why she had been imprisoned she answered "I have broken the vow of chastity" but pointing to the Sisters, in great excitement she said "But they are not angels". The Lady Superior said that the Nun had been kept in close confinement by order of the physician because of her unsound mind. This physician had died in 1848 and the present physician who had practised for seven years had never seen Barbara Ubryk. Such treatment in the opinion of the doctors is sufficient to drive a person mad. On account of the importance of the case the attorney in general has taken the matter in hand. The exasperation of the people knows no bounds. It is stated that the Bishop intends to dissolve the Convent.

Fatal Balloon Accident

A shocking fatality took place last Saturday afternoon in connection with a balloon ascent made from Eckington a short time previously by an aeronaut, whose name is stated to be Foster. The ascent was one of the leading features of the opening of a new market at Eckington by Mrs. Simpson, who is known as "The Derby Butcher", and took place soon after three o'clock. The balloon being soon carried by a north west wind in the direction of Worksop it was presently lost sight of. Later in the day the news reached Eckington that an accident had happened to the aeriel traveller, and it was subsequently gathered that the unfortunate man in endeavouring to descend near the village of Carlton in Lindrick, had been precipitated out of the car and killed on the spot.

TERRIBLE OUTRAGE—SHEFFIELD

On Monday, last week, at the Sheffield Hospital, Mr. Laycock one of the Borough justices, and Mr. Jackson the chief constable, were present while the depositions were taken of Thomas O'Rourke, a labourer, who was assaulted by his wife Bridget O'Rourke. O'Rourke said he lived at No. 5 Trippett Lane, Sheffield, and on Saturday night at half-past eleven, some words occurred between him and his wife about his wages. While they were quarelling Bridget suddenly seized the lamp and threw it at him. **His clothes were saturated in parraffin and he was immediately enveloped in flames. His face and chest were terribly burned and in trying to untie a scarf around his neck his hands were also badly burnt.** Both were sober at the time and had been married about forty years. The woman who is in custody when asked if she had anything to say replied "I only wish him God's blessing." She was remanded.

TERRIBLE OUTRAGE AT SHEFFIELD.

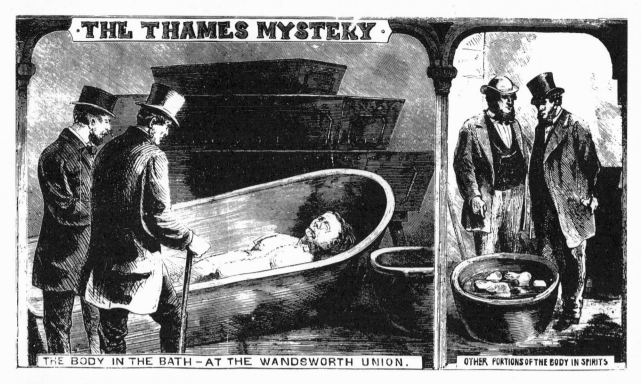

THE THAMES MYSTERY

THE BODY IN THE BATH – AT THE WANDSWORTH UNION.

OTHER PORTIONS OF THE BODY IN SPIRITS

THAMES MYSTERY—Murder and mutilation of a woman

As yet there is no evidence that the Police are on the track of the murderer in this mysterious case. With great patience the officers have carried out the story of each missing woman who has been reported to them as appearing as the deceased is supposed to have looked and it is mournful to reflect upon by the amount of accounts of women being missing, that there are many missing from home.

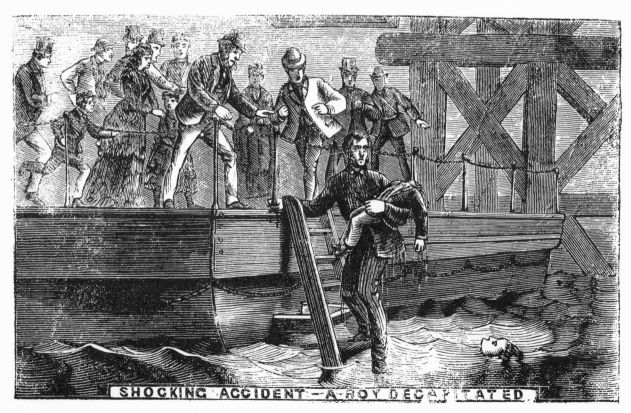

SHOCKING ACCIDENT – A BOY DECAPITATED

There is a new theory and it is certainly worth mentioning for the sake of its novelty. It certainly savours strongly of the Poe school of ideas, but it is not wanting in force. Given shortly, it is an account of the escaped criminal lunatics from Broadmoor Asylum—men it will be remembered of murderous propensities—with the outrages of late upon life in the west. It is said that Blagrove is thought to be at Staines or the neighbourhood, and there are not wanting those who have pictured the possibility of his hiding along the islands of Battersea Park, and thus securing a place remote from observation for the perpetuation of a crime which required strength of body, the deepest cunning, and a brutal disregard for all human feeling.

SAVED BY A KITE

A most remarkable escape from death occurred a few days ago, the fact being as follows:

"A little boy aged about ten years had an extraordinary escape from death at Maidstone a few days ago. He was flying a large kite on an open space at the west end of the town. When stepping backwards he fell into a quarry forty feet deep, to the great horror of some persons walking close by. Fortunately for the little fellow the string of his kite was around his wrist, and so instead of being dashed to pieces, he escaped with a few bruises, being in reality more frightened than hurt. The kite, acting as a parachute, effectually broke the force of the youngster's fall.

SHOCKING ACCIDENT
A boy decapitated

On Wednesday a fatal accident took place in which a porter and a little boy lost their lives. The boy went down to the pier to see the despatch of the steamer across the pier and for some unexplained reason he got too near the sliding luggage lifts and was struck in such a manner that he had his head completely severed from his body. Rawlins the porter who rushed to the rescue of the boy was also struck by the cage and crushed to death.

DEATH
IN A BATHING MACHINE

Two melancholy instances of the uncertainty of human life occurred last week. In both cases the victims were ladies. On Thursday last week, Mrs. Sylvester, the wife of an English merchant, was bathing in the vicinity of Dieppe, and while in the water she was observed by her friends to throw up her arms. In another moment she disappeared beneath the surface. What rendered this the more surprising was that she was not out of her depth. The screams of her female companions brought a boatman and a bathing woman to her assistance. The former succeeded in finding Mrs. Sylvester, who was at once carried into the bathing machine. She gave a faint sigh and expired almost immediately. Death resulted, according to the medical testimony, from fatty degeneration of the heart. The unfortunate lady leaves a husband and three children to mourn the loss of an exemplary wife and mother.

DEATH IN A BATHING MACHINE.

MURDER AND SUICIDE AT SALFORD

On Wednesday afternoon an inquest was held in the White Lion Public House, Wood Street, Salford, touching the death of Mary Ann Donoghue who was murdered by her husband on the morning of the previous day.

Mrs. Johnson said she was the wife of John Joseph Johnson, sawyer, residing in Wood Street, Salford. She had known the deceased and her husband for seven months, having lived next door to them during that time. On Wednesday morning, about five minutes to seven o'clock she saw Donoghue standing at the end of the entry adjoining her house. He said "Mrs. Johnson I am waiting on you". She asked what for and he replied she had been kind to his children and asked her to come and have a glass with him out of respect for what she had done to them. She refused and he pressed her she should have a glass of something although it should only be water. At last she and two neighbours consented to go to Mr. McGee's vaults with him and as soon as he got into the public house he called for four glasses of whiskey hot. While he was in the vaults he stated that he was a ruined man and his wife had turned his children against him in the sight of God and man and that he had lost his work through her. While drinking his glass he said "this man will soon be well; he will soon be ended". Witness did not know to whom he referred but he began to cry remarking that no one ever saw him shed tears before. When he finished his glass he went away bidding them good morning and saying that that was the eleventh one he had had that day. He seemed intoxicated. Witness and the other two women left the public house immediately afterwards and when she got opposite Donoghue's house she heard him upstairs, the window being open.

The door was shut and she heard the deceased call out "Oh Tom don't" and immediately after-afterwards "Oh good God what is this for?" Witness returned to the other two women whom she had left in the street and was telling them what she had heard when Donoghue came out of the house with no clothing on but his trousers and a flannel singlet. The latter he pulled off and showing them his side, which was streaming with blood, he said "this life is lost through an evil woman". Witness asked him who had done that and he replied (putting out his hand) "this hand has done it". He went back to his house and called out as he was entering "I am a broken hearted man through an evil woman". He then asked her to go for a policeman as he wanted to die. Witness went and told two policemen who proceeded to the house.

Police Constable Barrington said that in consequence of information which came to the Police Office in Salford on Wednesday morning he and another officer proceeded to the house No. 33 Wood Street, and there he saw Donoghue, the prisoner, sitting in a chair and blood flowing from a wound in his left side. Two women cried out "where is his wife". Witness proceeded upstairs and there found her lying on the floor in her nightdress, with her face down-

MURDER & ATTEMPTED SUICIDE AT SALFORD

ATTEMPTED WIFE MURDER AT BRIGHTON

wards. There was a pool of blood underneath her left side and by appearance she was dead. He went downstairs again and found that Donoghue had fallen from his chair and with the assistance of a few others had him conveyed to the Dispensary. After that he went for Dr. Stocks who examined the woman and pronounced her to be dead. He found the knife (produced) lying on the floor near the prisoner. There was nobody in the house but two children. He did not hear Donoghue speak after he entered the house, except something to the effect he would like to see his little boy.

Mrs. Cotterill said she lived in Wood Street and had known the deceased and her husband for about four years. For the last two years they had lived very unhappily together, the deceased during that time having given way to drinking. About five years ago she left her husband altogether taking the eldest boy with her. She came back on Monday night and witness heard them quarrelling and using bad language to each other in the house. She had never seen Donoghue intoxicated but twice during the time she had known him. Witness thought deceased was jealous

and that that had something to do with the unhappy life they led. She did not know that Donoghue had been out of employment. He had been working last week but not this.

Mr. A. W. Stocks, Surgeon, said he was called on Wednesday morning to the house of the deceased and there found her lying dead upon the floor. On examining the body he discovered

four wounds from which blood flowed. Since then he had made a post mortem examination of the body. Any of the wounds might have been committed by the knife produced.

The jury returned a verdict of "Wilful Murder" against Donoghue, who still remains in the Salford Dispensary but is in an improving condition.

ATTEMPTED WIFE MURDER

Attack by a husband on his wife in Upper-Market Street, Brighton.

At Hove Police-court, adjoining Brighton, on Wednesday last week a hand-chairman named T. Tuffnell, aged 48, residing at 18, Upper Market Street West, was brought up on a charge of attempting to murder his wife. The prisoner had been for many years past a very dissipated fellow, and frequently ill-used his wife. On Tuesday night, on his wife remonstrating with him for striking her in the street, he took from a nail in the bedroom in which they were seated a hatchet, and struck her over the head, inflicting a serious wound. The poor woman at the time had her youngest boy in her arms, who with herself was covered with blood. Her little girl immediately ran for assistance, and after some neighbours had come to the rescue medical aid was procured. Mr. Curtis, a surgeon, was afraid the wound would prove fatal. The prisoner expressed a wish that he had done for her, and also that he had killed himself. The magistrates remanded him to the 14th inst. The poor woman yet lies in a precarious state.

◆◆◆

A WOMAN RAISED FROM THE DEAD

A miracle is alleged to have been wrought at the village of Maunch Chunk in Pennsylvania. A lady, by name of Miss Amelia Greth, has, it is asserted, been raised from the dead by Father Heinan, a German Catholic Priest at Maunch Chunk. Miss Greth, according to her own account, was enabled through a communiication from her guardian angel, to predict her own death from consumption on the 2nd inst. but the prediction was accompanied by the gratifying announcement that she would be restored to life by a miracle, would get up from her death bed, attend mass, and return from church cured of all ailments. On the day mentioned, Miss Greth died accordingly, and her remains were viewed by 7,000 persons, who were permitted to pass through the room in which the corpse was lying. After Miss Greth had been dead for about an hour Father Heinan, who had attended her in her last moments, announced, amid the most profound silence, that he was about to "call her". **He then cried "Amelia" and, there being no response, shouted her name again in a loud voice, upon which Miss Greth immediately came to life then asked for a shawl and was accommodated with a sealskin jacket which a lady who stood by the bedside took off and placed on her shoulders.** She then walked alone and quite rapidly to church, followed by an immense concourse of people in a state of wild excitement.

When she arrived at the church Father Heinan preached two sermons—one in German, the other in English—and on the conclusion of the service Miss Greth returned to her room apparently strong and hearty. She has since been interviewed by several reporters; but as she is not permitted to describe her sensations during the time she was dead, her revelations were confined chiefly to details as to her health, which seems to have been far from satisfactory.

SUICIDE BY A GUILLOTINE

An inquest was held on Friday week on the body of a French Artisan who committed suicide under the following circumstances:

Mr. John Wilson stated that deceased had lodged with him for twelve months, and was apparently independent when he took the apartments. Latterly he seemed to be pressed for money and a fortnight

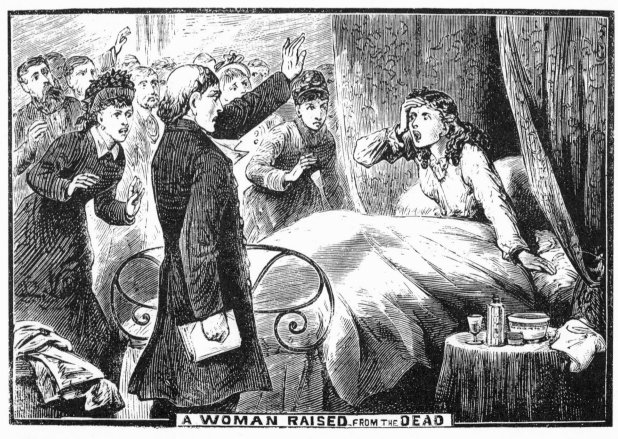

A WOMAN RAISED FROM THE DEAD

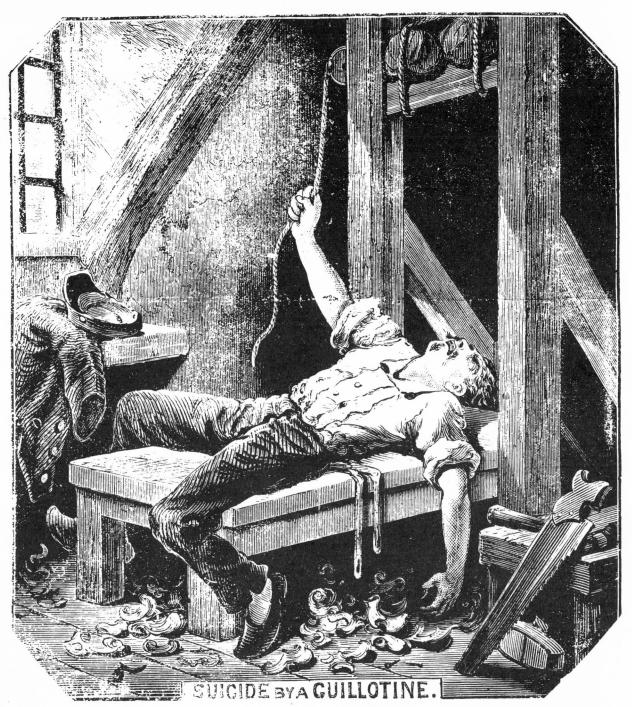

SUICIDE BY A GUILLOTINE.

ago told witness he was an artisan who had saved money for the purpose of going into business.

The previous Saturday he brought home two large planks of wood and a large double handled knife, such as is used by tanners for scraping the hair off skins, but no notice was taken of it, witness thinking it was for model-making. On Monday his suicide was discovered his head having been cut off by a guillotine. The two planks had been used as uprights at the top of which the knife had been placed. Grooves had been cut in the inner side of the planks for the knife to run easily and two heavy stones were bound to the upper side of the knife to give it weight. By means of the pulley he had drawn up the knife and let it fall on his throat, the head being cut clean off.

Confirmatory evidence having been given the Jury returned a verdict of unsound mind.

ATTACK UPON A BOY BY A DOG

William Glines, aged six and a half years, of 50, Castle Street, Longacre, got into the wrong passage of a house, when a bull dog seized him by one of his cheeks, and tore nearly the whole of the flesh from the bone. His shrieks brought assistance and the wound was promptly sewn up and cauterised, but his recovery is considered to be doubtful.

SUICIDE FROM WATERLOO BRIDGE

An inquest was held on Friday evening at St. Martin's Vestry room near Charing Cross, respecting the death of a woman unknown, and who was supposed to be about forty years old. The evidence given was to the effect that on Monday last, the deceased went to the toll-man on duty at Waterloo Bridge and begged that he would permit her to pass without paying. She had no money she said. The tollman refused, and the woman, seeing some gentlemen approaching the bridge, asked them for money and obtained a penny. She then passed the toll-gate. When she was about half way across the bridge, she was seen to take off her bonnet, and suddenly mounting the side of the bridge she leaped into the river. As she descended her head came in contact with a buttress and was literally smashed. The body was recovered shortly afterwards and it was seen that the woman had no boots on, and that her clothing was miserably poor. A verdict was given to the effect that she had committed suicide whilst she was temporarily insane.